Discovering Shropshire Towns

Dorothy Nicolle

Blue Hills Press

Guiding is a marvellous occupation.
You meet the friendliest of people.
You visit fascinating places.
You learn such interesting things -
particularly when asked questions to which
you don't know the answer!
This book is dedicated to all those who have
joined me on tours in Shropshire and beyond.
Thank you for making it all such a joy.

Front cover photographs, clockwise from top left -
Shrewsbury, the Tudor coat of arms on the Old Market Hall
Ellesmere, St Mary's Church
Ludlow, Prince Arthur window in St Lawrence's Church
Ironbridge, the Merrythought Teddy Bear Museum
Bishop's Castle, the Square

Back cover photograph -
Ludlow, Broad Gate

ISBN 978-0-9560293-2-4

Published by –
Blue Hills Press, 32 Chapel Street, Wem, Shropshire SY4 5ER
www.bluehillspress.co.uk

Printed by Cambrian Printers, Llanbadarn Road,
Aberystwyth SY23 3TN

Contents

Key to town maps

The maps in this book are not drawn to scale. They have been considerably simplified to emphasise the route that each walk follows.

Although car parks are shown on each map it is not advisable that drivers should use the maps in the book in order to drive to them – some narrow lanes that appear on the maps are not suitable for car traffic nor, for example, are one-way roads shown.

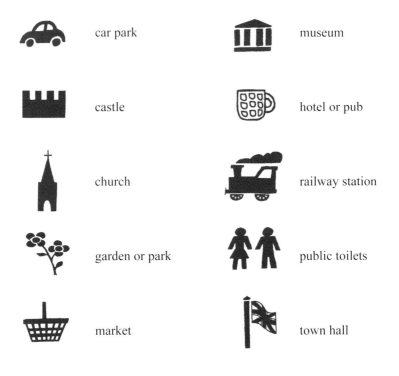

car park

museum

castle

hotel or pub

church

railway station

garden or park

public toilets

market

town hall

Introduction

Most walk books make an effort to ensure that the walks are circular so you don't get lost. My attitude is different. I hope you will get lost because only then will you become a true explorer. Consequently, although one or two walks are circular, most are not. I hope this encourages you to make your own detours and discoveries, hence the use of the word "discovering" in the book's title.

The walks are all short in terms of distance. Walking briskly, some would take less than 15 minutes. However, do ensure that you have plenty of time to linger and visit places along the way.

In times past special arrangements were seldom made for those who were disabled. Today we are more thoughtful but it does mean that there are still parts of each town that are difficult for many people to manage. Sadly, this is often the case in the more interesting areas where there are steps, cobbles or simply steep hills.

Take care as you go - it's easy to follow walks such as these with your nose in a book, only looking up once you reach a stop. In areas with busy traffic this is asking for trouble, so do please keep your wits about you as you explore.

Now, go and discover for yourself Shropshire's delightful and fascinating towns.

Dorothy Nicolle
2009

Bishop's Castle

The walk in Bishop's Castle starts beside the church and will finish at the top of the hill.

Dedicated to St John the Baptist, there has been a church here since at least 1291. Nothing remains of that early church (except for a doorway now in the wall leading to the former vicarage) as it was burnt down first in 1592 and again during the time of the Civil War. Despite its Norman appearance the tower is thought by some to date from the 17th century rebuilding, probably using much of the original stone. That church was then totally remodelled by the Victorians. Today we regularly complain when buildings are altered. It was the same in the late 1800s when local people complained about "the vandals of 1860".

Campanologists may be interested to learn that the church tower houses a peal of six bells dating mostly to the early 1700s. The treble is inscribed with the words "When you us ring we'll sweetly call".

Before setting off on the walk take a last look at the clock on the church tower. It's only got one hand and local people will tell you that this explains the slower, more relaxed pace of life in Bishop's Castle.

From the church gate cross over the road and walk straight ahead,

along Church Street. The Six Bells pub, a former coaching inn, sits on the left beside what was once a main road linking mid-Wales with London. For all that Bishop's Castle is only a small town (it's population is around 1,700 people) it has within it two breweries and this is the first of them.

I love the many coloured buildings of this town – all the colours of the rainbow are to be found on buildings here giving the town a happy and youthful atmosphere. That's not to say it's only the young who have painted their houses - far from it. In fact I often feel that it's as if all the flower-people and hippies from the 1960s have settled here and brought their love of colour with them. Notice that one house in the row on the right is called the Tan House, reminding us that here once was a tannery.

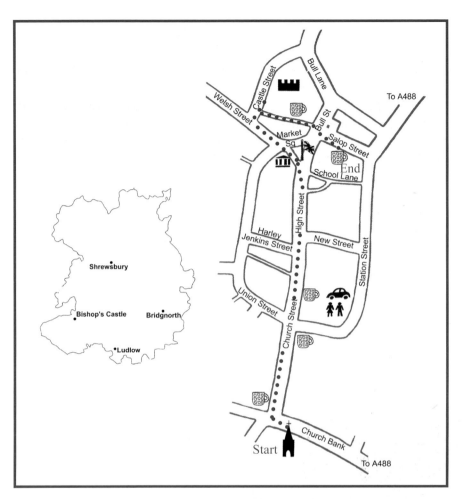

When visiting churches it is usually the case that the most interesting things are to be found inside. Here it is different – it's the churchyard that contains the real finds. Beside the west door there's the grave of a Frenchman, Louis Paces, who was captured during the Peninsular Wars and subsequently died here in 1814.

The most poignant discovery, though, is that of an African slave, known only as "ID" who died in 1801. His grave (pictured) is near the road to the north of the churchyard. Its inscription is now virtually illegible which is a pity because it reminds us that "God hath made of one blood all Nations of men".

Walk up Church Street and stop beside the old timber-framed house with the red-brick infill. Known as the Harp House, it served as the Harp Inn until 1902. Notice the way in which the upper floors of the building extend slightly beyond the ground floor – this is known as *jettying* and is a frequent feature of early timber buildings. Although the size of the plot is pre-determined, by building a house to the limit of the plot lines and then extending the upper floors, a considerable amount of extra floor space is obtained.

Next, stop just beyond the Boar's Head, a pub which has had a licence since at least 1642. You have now reached Station Street. It was once intended that this street would lead to the railway station but the railway never came to the town. The original plan for the railway line was that it should link Craven Arms with Montgomery, passing through Bishop's Castle on the way. Unfortunately, the whole venture was somewhat speculative and the company ran out of money before it reached here, stopping near Lydham. It's probably no wonder, therefore, that the line was never a commercial success. Yet it still managed to run for some 70 years, before being closed in 1935.

Continue towards the next pub, the King's Head. Just before you reach it notice the small lane off to the right; it leads to the present-day cattle market, once the site for the town's May Fair. Bishop's Castle has always been an important trading centre, attracting people in the past not only from the surrounding countryside but from deep into central Wales as well. The town's weekly market dates back to 1292. Normally charters for markets

---

Rotten Bishop's Castle

Bishop's Castle has the somewhat dubious distinction of once being a rotten borough. In medieval times the real power in the country rested with major landowners and few ordinary individuals had the vote. The selection of MPs representing towns was controlled by local landowners. Bishop's Castle may well have had two representatives in Parliament but few of the local people had any real choice in who these representatives actually were.

As time went by some towns grew in size while others declined. This was particularly the case once the Industrial Revolution began with new towns growing that had no parliamentary representation. By the 1800s it became apparent that the whole system needed to be reorganised. By then Bishop's Castle's importance had declined yet the little town still had two representatives in Parliament. There were a number of such towns up and down the country and they came to be known as rotten boroughs.

Eventually, in the 1830s, the Reform Acts were passed totally reorganising the electoral system throughout the country. As a result Bishop's Castle retained one of its MPs so that, until later reforms in 1965, the town continued as the smallest borough in England.

would have been given by the monarch but in Bishop's Castle it was the church that was all-powerful and so it was the Bishop of Hereford, Bishop Richard Swinfield, who gave the town permission to hold this particular weekly market.

While you are beside the King's Head take the time to look up the street. It's not just the colourful buildings that attract notice. Another thing that strikes visitors to Bishop's Castle is the regularity of the street layout. Indeed, if you were to take a measuring rod with you as you walk along Church Street and High Street, you would soon see that the facades of each house measure very much the same (about 33 feet, or a *rod* as it was known in medieval times). Occasionally you will see a much larger house but, again, careful measurement usually reveals that this is a multiple of two or three rods. All this comes about because the town of Bishop's Castle was originally a planned town with plots being carefully measured before being sold or rented out.

These plots were all relatively long and narrow and a thorough exploration of the town soon reveals that this early layout still dominates the street plan. Each of those early plots faced onto the High Street and extended to an entrance on a street behind – those back streets still survive as Union Street and Station Street. As individual plots they seem enormous to us. But, in an age when land was plentiful and each household  consisted of much more than a family unit of parents and 2.4 children, where space was required for pigs and chickens, workshops and stores, they make much more sense.

Cross over New Street. Notice the chemist's shop just beside the junction – it was once a primary school, you can see the sign for the school entrance over the doorway on the right. The school was founded with a bequest of £200 left by a lady called Mary Morris who asked that the school be known as *Mr Wright's Charity School* in memory of her first husband.

Just as the High Street starts to steepen look out for a little lane on the right – School Lane. It's down here that you will find the Bishop's Castle Rail and Transport Museum. It's run by volunteers and so opening times are limited.

Facing School Lane, on the opposite side of the street, is Porch House. Built in 1564 it has been described as "one of the most important and sumptuous houses in the town". It's now used for bed & breakfast accommodation. The first thing to catch your eye will probably be the modern art sculpture that sits in front of the building – *Titania*, by a local artist, Rog Williams. However, look also for the carvings that adorn the building itself; some are original and some are obviously very modern but they all sit together very happily.

The top of the High Street was once much broader than it is today, to accommodate a market area just below the castle which we will see shortly. That old market is remembered in the name of the street beyond which is still known as Market Square. Today the Town Hall (dating from 1760) sits in the centre of that old market space, dominating the High Street and with an excellent view all the way down the street.

Walk past the Town Hall along the little street to the left known as The Cobbles. Extending into the street, just ahead, is the House on Crutches. Here we have a jettied house like the one we saw earlier but, in this case, the jetties have been extended so far out that they need additional support, hence the *crutches*. The building is now the most delightful little town museum. It is run by volunteers so that opening times are limited but, if it is open, you just must go in and explore. Be warned, however; like any house of its period many of its floors are uneven and there are different levels with little flights of steps between.

Just beyond the House on Crutches go up the Cobbles into Market Square. All the buildings on the north side of the street are built within the area once used for the market, just outside the castle walls. Looking to your right you can't help but notice the terracotta coloured building at the end – this is Yarborough House; a specialist shop for classical records and second-hand books and CDs.

But instead, turn left into Welsh Street, along which drovers once brought their cattle to market, and then almost immediately go right into Castle Street. As you walk up Castle Street look out for a small flight of steps in the stone wall on the right. This takes you up to the site of Bishop's Castle's castle. Here you will find an information board detailing the history of the castle and, just beyond it, a section of the old outer bailey wall.

The name "Bishop's Castle" reminds us that there was once a castle here belonging to a bishop. Today, however, all that remains of that castle are little bits of wall in some private houses and the section of stonework that stands here.

This land once belonged to an old Saxon lord named Egwin Shakehead. Egwin suffered from the palsy and went to visit St Ethelbert's shrine at Hereford where he was miraculously cured. Consequently, when he died, he left his estate here to the cathedral at Hereford – hence the *bishop* in the town's name. Incidentally, the town's Welsh name was Y Trefysgob meaning "the town of the bishops".

There wasn't a castle here at first although, presumably, there may well have been a small settlement of some sort. It was a Norman Bishop of Hereford, Robert Losinga, who built the first castle, mentioned in records dating to 1087. As with so many other castles hereabouts, it wouldn't have been long before local people gravitated towards the castle for safety in turbulent times or simply to trade with inhabitants so that to set up a market would have been an obvious course of action for the local landowners, Hereford Cathedral. Thus, by around 1127, the layout of the town that we saw as we walked up the hill, was being laid out.

The House on Crutches is one of many buildings in Shropshire where you can still see carpenters' marks. On the timbers on the front wall you will find Roman numerals cut into the wood. The timbers for houses such as this would have been prepared in a yard elsewhere, measured and fitted and then, before being transported onto the building site, they would have been numbered so that the house could be erected as quickly as possible. It's relatively rare, however, to find them on the front of the building, a part that would usually have been reserved for decoration.

11

Like the rest of Shropshire's castles, this was one of the network of castles built to protect the English border area from Welsh incursions. The first wooden castle here was rebuilt in stone in 1167, a very necessary defence at a time when the Welsh were regularly attacking and "ravaging and slaying and burning and plundering without mercy". In the 1280s the castle was extensively rebuilt and it was around this time that we first see the town being referred to in documents as Bishop's Castle.

It survived as a habitable castle until the 1530s, by which time the two nations of England and Wales had become united. During Queen Elizabeth I's reign a survey of all crown possessions was carried out. At this time the castle still had 15 habitable rooms, a prison, a dovecote and gardens and parks. In the early 1600s it was sold and from this time it began to fall into disrepair but it wasn't finally destroyed until the time of the Civil War when, in 1644, the town was attacked and what little was left of the castle, together with a number of houses in the town, were burnt. By then, however, it would seem that many of the timbers in the original castle building had already been recycled for use in local houses.

From here retrace your steps down the hill towards Welsh Street but turn left along a little lane which takes you to the car park of the Castle Hotel. Stopping in the car park there's very little left to suggest that there was ever a castle here apart from the name of the hotel which was built in 1719 (there's a date on the far side). This area was once occupied by an outer bailey while the original area of the motte, behind the hotel, is now used for a bowling green. The bowling club dates from at least the 1700s though no-one knows for sure. Indeed, the earliest records of the game of bowls in England date back to the 1200s. By late medieval times the game had become so popular and so many young men preferred it to doing their archery practice, that a law was passed in 1541 stating that people of the working class could only play bowls during the Christmas holiday season.

Walk past the hotel and down the slope beyond; continue straight ahead and you will find a delightful spot in which to sit and watch the world go by. Once a bustling part of the town, it was here that the market hall once stood – it was demolished in 1951 and all that remains of it is the finely carved coat of arms.

From the market place continue walking along Salop Street and, almost immediately, you will see on your right the Three Tuns pub. This is where our tour comes to an end. Like the Six Bells near the church, this pub is one of the few in the country that brews its own beer and it even has its own four-storey Victorian brew-house, sitting rather like a tall tower beside the pub itself. This is a Grade II listed building as such brew houses attached to pubs are rare. Also very scarce these days are pubs that can claim to have been brewing ale for over 300 years – although there was a brief break of around 18 months a few years ago, the Three Tuns has been brewing beer here since at least 1642. A fine place to finish our tour.

The arms are those of the Earls of Powis who owned vast swathes of land around this area. The elephant depicted here is interesting because it is a link with Robert Clive of India whose son married a daughter of the Earl of Powis and later inherited the title for himself. As for Robert Clive, although born in the north of the county (near Market Drayton), he subsequently bought the nearby estate at Walcot Hall.

Bridgnorth

This walk wends its way through the High Town area of Bridgnorth. If you want to follow the entire route the walk is not for the fainthearted as, at one point, it goes down to the bottom of the hill and then there are steps to climb back up again. However, you can cheat and come back up the hill using the cliff railway instead or, if you prefer, you can leave out this loop altogether.

The tour starts at the southern end of the town on Castle Hill Walk just beside the point where the steps come up from New Road. Standing here you get a marvellous view of the valley and countryside around Bridgnorth and it immediately becomes apparent just why the town sits where it does.

For all that it's long been one of the most important towns in Shropshire it's interesting to note that there was no settlement here in Saxon times, certainly the place doesn't get a mention in the Domesday Book of 1086. There was a fording point on the River Severn but that was a couple of miles to the south of the town at Quatford. That's not to say that no-one had ever occupied the site – the hill we are on is made from a very soft sandstone that crops out on both sides of the river and is riddled with caves. One cave on the other side of the river, known as the Hermitage, is said to have been occupied by a man called Ethelred, the hermit grandson of King Alfred.

The site was recognised early on for its defensive capabilities. In the 890s a number of Vikings stayed here. They had been trapped in the Thames Valley by King Alfred's army and their longships burnt so they fled in this direction, staying for the winter before they could get away. Presumably, with its high ground, they would have used the site we are standing on but it's also understood that the hillock that you can see to the south-west, just beyond the railway station and known as Panpudding Hill, is where they had one of their encampments. Unfortunately, the site was used some 200 years later as a besieging camp when Henry I attacked the castle. To the frustration of modern archaeologists, any Viking archaeology has been thoroughly destroyed.

Actually not new at all – the road was built in 1786. Until that point the only access into the town for vehicles was up and down narrow Cartway.

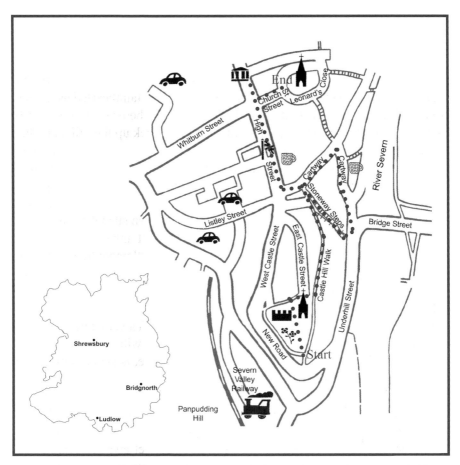

Start the tour by walking through the gardens. These were laid out to commemorate Queen Victoria's Diamond Jubilee in 1897. Walk past the bandstand, and stop when you reach the leaning tower of the old castle.

In 1066 when the Normans arrived in England they set about subduing the entire country. At first they ignored this site entirely, just ensuring that they controlled the river crossing. These lands were given to one of King William's generals, Roger de Montgomery. Montgomery subsequently died and his son, Robert de Belleme, inherited. By all accounts, in an age when warlords were expected to be fierce, Robert was notorious for his extreme cruelty, often carrying out tortures himself when it would have been normal to give such tasks to henchmen. It's said that he once deliberately starved a number of his prisoners to death, his excuse being that, as it was Lent, they shouldn't have any food anyway.

It was Robert who built the first castle on this site. Having built it, he then used it as a stronghold from which to rebel against King Henry I. Henry came here and besieged the castle; Robert was eventually captured and exiled back to Normandy, losing his English estates.

From this time Bridgnorth's castle remained, for much of its life, under royal control. Over time it was extended so that, at its largest, the main castle covered the entire area where the gardens and church stand, with an additional outer bailey now occupied by the houses along East Castle Street. Despite the fact that it sits on the western side of Shropshire, this castle was one of the major castles protecting the English-Welsh border, and was used largely as a support castle for others further west.

By the time of the Tudors the castle had fallen into disrepair. Then in the 1640s came the Civil War and it was hurriedly refortified by Royalist forces. In 1646 Bridgnorth was captured by a Parliamentarian army who turned their attention on the castle. Their siege was a long, drawn out affair with cannon fire from both sides. One "lucky" shot on the part of the Royalists hit the Parliamentarian arsenal which had been housed in St Leonard's Church so that not only was the church blown up but the explosion started a fire that destroyed much of the town as well.

The Parliamentarians, realising that the castle's inhabitants could withstand a siege for months, then decided on an alternative tactic. Remembering how soft the sandstone beneath the castle was, they decided to tunnel underneath and dig out a hole which they would then stuff with gunpowder and use to blow up the entire hillside. The man put in charge of this project was a Colonel Lavington – over a period of 26 days his men dug a tunnel through the hillside. It's known as Lavington's Hole and the entrance (now blocked up) can still be seen from Underhill Street. Fortunately for those in the castle, word of what was planned reached them and they wisely surrendered. The castle was subsequently blown up from above ground which is why all that you see today is this alarmingly tilted ruin. It's lean is greater than that of the Leaning Tower of Pisa!

Now walk under the ruin and turn right. Stop when you reach the entrance of St Mary Magdalene Church. Within the old castle there would have been a chapel of some sort on this site. This church, however, only dates from 1792. It was built by Thomas Telford and is a marvellous example of churches of the period – light, spacious and very simple but elegant in its design. If you have the chance, do take the opportunity to look inside.

Before moving on from here, turn around and look up East Castle Street. The writer, Edith Pargeter, once described it as "one of the most urbane and gracious town streets in England". Sitting within the bounds of the castle, one building dates from that early time – it's No 18 and was the former castle governor's house. Most of the houses here, however, were built after the town had recovered following the Civil War fire and date from the 18th century.

Continue walking beyond the church and down the steps to reach Castle Hill Walk. Turn left and walk until you reach a point where the lane bends slightly opening up a wonderful view looking north and east. When he visited the town in 1642, Charles I stood here and described it as "the finest view in my dominion".

The view is dominated by the River Severn below, the longest river in Great Britain. Apart from the traffic passing over the bridge the riverside looks quiet these days. In the past it would have been a hive of activity as this was a major trading route with boats carrying goods up and downstream. It wasn't just used by small boats either – many that went through here carried goods around the coast to London, some are known to have traded with places as far afield as the Baltic and South America. Sea-going ships were even built in Bridgnorth.

With the coming of the railway and then of motorised traffic, the river trade came to an end. It finished rather ignominiously when, in 1895, a barge hit the bridge and sank – so ended a long tradition.

The bridge is, of course, the reason for the town's name - the bridge to the north of the ford. For a long time after the first bridge was built here in the early 1300s the town was known simply as *Brigge*. The present bridge was designed by Thomas Telford and was once a toll bridge. It was narrower in those days, being widened in the 1960s to accommodate present-day traffic.

Before moving on, can you see the clock tower on the other side of the bridge? The land just beyond it was once the site of John Hazledine's iron foundry and it was here, in 1808, that Richard Trevithick's *Catch-me-who-can* was built, the world's first passenger pulling steam engine. It was transported by ship from here to London where it was exhibited with people having rides for one shilling a time, so ushering in the age of the steam train.

Another train, although not run by steam, is the cliff railway that you will see ahead of you as you turn the corner. It was built in 1892 and worked on a water balance system – there were two carriages, each of which had a water tank beneath it; the carriage at the top would have its tank filled with water while the water was emptied from the carriage at the bottom. The heavier carriage would then act as a counterbalance to the lighter carriage as they moved up and down on the tracks. The system was changed to electricity in 1940. Today it is the only surviving inland cliff railway in the country.

Continue straight on to the end of the walkway beyond the cliff railway entrance. It is at this point that you have to decide whether or not you wish to walk the loop down the hill and back again. If you want to take the full walk, then go to the end of the street and turn right to start walking down Cartway.

The loop

This steep street was once the main route in and out of Bridgnorth; in fact for a long time it was the only street wide enough for wheeled, horse-drawn vehicles to use.

The Cartway bends sharply to the right. Just before this point you will see, on your left, an unusual bricked up wall – behind it are caves that were used as houses until 1856 when they were blocked up. The sandstone hills are pockmarked with little caves and many are still in use today as garages and stores, though not as houses anymore. The caves make excellent stores having an even temperature throughout the year. At one time, Bridgnorth was famous for its "cave ales".

> There's a little rhyme
> that goes -
>
> Shrewsbury town for biscuits,
> Whitchurch for cheese,
> Much Wenlock for pretty girls
> And Bridgnorth for fleas.
>
> The mention of fleas here is said
> to be a reference to the fleas that
> infested the caves in which so
> many local people once lived.

Speaking of ales, continue on down the street until you reach the Black Boy pub. Cartway was once lined with pubs – the 1851 census tells us that there were six lodging houses and five inns in this street alone. All types of people lodged here – watermen, farm labourers, carpet workers and, when the railway was being built, railway navvies. They were a rough crowd and the street didn't exactly have a good reputation in those days.

A little further down, also on the left, there's a fine timber-framed mansion. This is known as Bishop Percy's House, after Thomas Percy, a grocer's son who was born here in 1729 and grew up to become Bishop of Dromore in Ireland. The house was built in 1580 and, believe it or not, the backyard was once used as an iron and brass foundry which strikes me as a rather risky business to carry out in the yard of a timber building!

Once at the bottom of Cartway you may like to take a little time to walk along Underhill Road and look for Lavington's Cave before climbing back to High Town. To return to High Town follow the signs for the cliff railway. You can then choose either to use the railway to return to the top or, if you are feeling energetic, take the steps that you will see just to the left – Stoneway Steps. Be warned – there are 178 steps but you can rest half way up when you reach the aptly named Theatre on the Steps – this was built as a Congregationalist chapel in the 18th century. A survey, taken in 1890, found that 3,000 people used the steps in one 12-hour period.

Continuing with the main walk

Reaching the top of the steps you find yourself on Castle Terrace beside the top of Cartway. This time turn left and walk to the High Street. There is a wide area of pavement beside the road junction where you can stand and look around. The area between here and the upper cliff railway station is where, in medieval times, there would have been walls and ditches surrounding the outer bailey of Bridgnorth Castle. You are now, finally, in the old town.

This street has served since the town's earliest days as the main market area. The control of a market was an essential source of income and one would have been established

Notice, just beyond the theatre, the attractive ironwork built over the alleyway – these are known as Pope's Spectacles. This isn't being irreverent; it's just that the man who owned the foundry where they were made was called John Pope. They were erected to act as buttresses to stop the walls from caving in.

soon after the castle was built. The town's first charter to hold a regular market was granted by Henry II in 1157 and Bridgnorth rapidly became one of the major markets in Shropshire. One reference states that in one day's trading in the late 1500s sales reached £10,000, a phenomenal sum of money for the times. In Victorian times, however, town planners decided that they wanted to move the market off the street and so had the New Market Building built – it's that over-ornate, multi-coloured brick building sitting on one corner. Their plan didn't work. Only one trader moved into the new building so that the market thrives in the street to this day.

Take your time as you wander up the street – there are many buildings worth a second glance. The Swan Hotel, for example, dates from the 1600s – there are records indicating that it was largely rebuilt after the 1646 fire and, indeed, some of the older timbers show signs of having been burnt.

Standing in the middle of the street is a building that was built from new following that fire – the Town Hall. There is a tradition that the timber part of the building sitting on the brick and stone base was once a barn in Much Wenlock. There is no evidence to prove this but, when people wanted to rebuild their town quickly after a fire it made sense to use whatever timber was readily available and I see no reason why timber from a sturdy barn shouldn't be used. It is well worth a visit (the entrance is on the left-hand side) – the former Council Chamber survives inside.

Now walk up towards the old stone North Gate and stop once again. This is the only survivor of five medieval gates into the town. Built in the 1200s it has been remodelled several times since then – the battlements, for example, only date from 1910! At one time, in the late 1800s, the building housed a school for "the education, clothing and apprenticing of 30 boys of the lower middle classes". Today it is home to a delightful little museum with a particularly fine collection of fire insurance plaques. Entrance to the museum is up the rather steep flight of stairs on the right.

To reach St Leonard's, where the tour ends, retrace your steps and turn left into Church Street. As you walk up this street notice the little garden on your left – this is a memorial garden to two people who were killed in their house here in a bombing raid in 1940. With only eight fatalities from bombing raids in the whole county, Shropshire was fortunate indeed.

Walk up towards St Leonard's Church. Before going into the church notice the building beyond it, on the right. Divided into three it once housed Bridgnorth Grammar School, the schoolmaster and the vicar of St Leonard's.

It's not known exactly when the school was founded but it was certainly in existence by 1547 when the schoolmaster was paid £8 a year.

Finally, look at the church. Thanks to the Parliamentarian soldiers who used the church to store their ammunition, we have no evidence of the earliest church on this site which would have dated from before 1250. Following the 1646 fire the church was hurriedly rebuilt, perhaps a bit too hurriedly because it needed a complete renovation in 1870 so that the church we see today is largely Victorian. Sadly, it is now redundant but it's still consecrated and open to the public, being used regularly for concerts and other events. The church contains some fine stained glass, early iron tombstones and, my own particular favourite, a memorial to a namesake of mine called Dorothy who is described as "a discreet woman" which always sets me wondering! Go and find it.

Richard Baxter, whose home this was for a short time, was born in the village of Eaton Constantine in Shropshire. Largely self-educated, he came here to act as curate before moving on to Kidderminster. He was one of the leading non-conformist preachers of his day but got into trouble in his later years when he was vociferous in his criticism not only of bishops within the Church of England but also of the ruling establishment.

He obviously had rather mixed views of the people of Bridgnorth once describing them as "ignorant and dead hearted" while on another occasion he called them his "dearly beloved friends". When the fire occurred in 1646 he wrote a letter to the townspeople saying the disaster was largely their own fault and "as the flames of war have consumed your houses, so may the Spirit of God consume the sin that was the cause".

Broseley

The *ley* in the name Broseley is an Anglo-Saxon term that tells us that the first settlement here would have been a simple clearing in a forest. Coming to this town from almost any direction it is still easy to imagine that the countryside here was once thickly wooded.

This tour begins beside All Saints Church in what was once the heart of the village although now it's very much on the edge. Broseley was listed in the Domesday Book of 1086 but the church wasn't mentioned; this doesn't mean that there was no church then as only those made of stone were listed in Domesday. Presumably there would have been a small, timber church of some sort to serve that early hamlet.

That early church was then replaced by a stone one in the early 1700s, dedicated to St Leonard. However, just over one hundred years later the church you see today was built at a cost of £9,000 and it was at this point that the dedication changed.

Before leaving the churchyard look out for Broseley Hall next door. This fine mansion was designed by Thomas Farnolls Pritchard. Pritchard, who was also involved in the design of the Iron Bridge, was born in Shrewsbury in 1723 and became one of the leading Shropshire architects of the period. Many examples of his work survive. Buildings he designed in Shropshire include the present Shrewsbury School (then a Foundling Hospital), the Lion Hotel in Shrewsbury and the Hosiers Almshouses in Ludlow as well as numerous private houses around the county.

It must be said, however, that in the mid 1800s the Hall was occupied for a short time by a Mrs Favell Lee Mortimer who wrote religious children's books and she once described it as "a dark mausoleum of a place".

Just outside the door of the church are some cast iron tombs. One flat one has anchors and ropes in the corners, giving it a nautical appearance although here it remembers a trowman, one of the bargemen who carried goods up and down the River Severn.

For the first few hundred years of its existence, Broseley survived only as the smallest of settlements – in fact, even as late as 1600 there were just 27 houses in the village. By then, a secondary settlement had begun to develop further west on what was then known as Cole Pitt Hill, a name that tells us a great deal about why this town grew at all.

Consequently, as we explore Broseley you will see none of the pretty little timber houses that you find in so many of the other towns of Shropshire. Instead, with a few notable exceptions, this is a town of lowly little artisan's cottages and workshops. For example, take a look at the two cottages you see

across the road as you leave the churchyard. It was in the workshop of Number 7, on the right, that the ironmaster, John Wilkinson, once had a mint producing coinage – notice the name of the house.

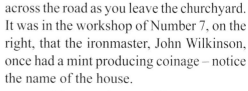

The next house of interest as you start to walk up Church Street, is hardly an artisan's cottage – known as The Lawns, it was the home of John Wilkinson himself. Wilkinson was a man who had immense influence here – in fact, it is thought that the idea of building an iron bridge may well have come from him. Born in Cumberland, he was the son of an iron founder. By the time Wilkinson arrived in Broseley he was already well established as an iron master and very wealthy. It's no exaggeration to say that the man was obsessed by iron. Not only was he involved in the building of the world's first iron bridge but he also built the world's first iron boat. It was said of him that he never wrote a letter without using the word "iron" in it somewhere. Then, when he died in 1808, he was buried in an iron coffin.

Continue along Church Street and this time, look out for Raddle Hall, on the right hand side near the junction with Foundry Lane. Built in the 1660s, it's thought to have been the first house in the town to be built from bricks. It was once the home of John

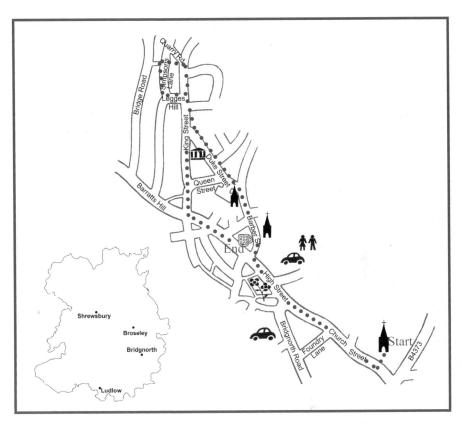

Randall who is now best known for his *History of Madeley*, published in 1880. Although he wrote a number of books on local history, he really ought to be remembered more for his artistic skills. He worked at the Coalport China factory as a ceramic artist, producing the most beautiful paintings, particularly of birds. Incidentally, he lived to be 100 years old, dying in 1910.

The influence of local industries is never far away once you start exploring Broseley. As you continue walking, look out next for a building that is known as the "Iron-topped House", also on the right hand side of the street. Its name comes about because even the rafters within the roof are made of iron.

Walk into the High Street and stop once you are opposite the green in the heart of the town. In the early 18th century this area was extremely mucky – it was then a flooded opencast coal pit, used also as a fish pond. It was filled in when the memorial gardens that you see here now were developed.

Just beyond the Memorial Gardens is the Victoria Hall. Now used for various communal activities within Broseley, when it was built in 1867 this building served as a meeting place for Plymouth Brethren. It was one of a number of non-conformist chapels established in Broseley. Broseley had meeting halls or chapels for Quakers, Congregationalists, Methodists, Baptists and this is typical of small industrial communities in the 1700s and 1800s throughout Britain. The development of new industries required men and women who were capable of making decisions for themselves and of thinking in new ways. This free-thinking inevitably led to them looking at all aspects of the world around them and questioning all that they saw, including their religious beliefs. Notice the decorative tiles on the gable end of the hall – these were given by the Maw family, manufacturers of fine tiles, who partly financed the building work.

When you reach the road junction with a small roundabout bear right and walk along Barber Street and then into Duke Street.

In Barber Street you pass the Roman Catholic church. Having just seen the connection with the Maw family at the Plymouth Brethren meeting hall it is interesting to consider that in fact the family home just outside Broseley, Benthall Hall, is famous for its association with Roman Catholics.

The house that sits between the junction of Duke Street and Cockshutt Lane (opposite the Methodist church) was once a pub, called the Lord Hill. Hill was the general whom the Duke of Wellington always said he "could trust". He made his name in the Peninsular War in the early 1800s and then also fought at Waterloo. Following the war many of his soldiers, retiring back

Now in the care of the National Trust, Benthall Hall dates from the 1500s. Carvings around the main entrance are said to represent Christ's wounds from the Crucifixion and may have been a secret sign to Roman Catholics at the time of their persecution.

to Shropshire, would have opened pubs using Hill's name on the sign and this is may well have been one of them as it was first licensed in 1821.

When you reach Queen Street on the left, walk down it until you see the house known as Hurst Lea on the left. It was here that the first meeting to discuss the building of an iron bridge took place.

Retrace your steps to return to Duke Street and continue to the Broseley Pipe Museum. Visiting this museum is a must – having been a pipe factory for 350 years it was abandoned in 1957. Reopened as a museum in 1996 it now looks as though the workers have just walked out of the door only five minutes ago, everything has been perfectly restored. It was once one of three pipe factories in the town. The pipes were made from local clay and exported all over the country. Very often the pipes were sold already filled with tobacco so that "to have a Broseley" was synonymous with having a smoke.

Never automatically believe all that you read on signs. The sign outside the museum tells us that Abraham Darby I was buried in the adjoining Quaker graveyard. In fact Darby was buried on another site in Broseley – this was later developed, at which time his and other graves were moved here.

From the pipe museum continue along Duke Street and then turn right into King Street. As you go, look out for the little tile-covered building on the left-hand side of the street. Your eye will be drawn to the myriad of different tiles of all types of patterns and colours and you will want to cross over the road to have a closer look. It was once a butcher's shop and is an absolute gem of a building. If you look inside the window, you will see the interior is similarly covered in tiles. Tile production was a major industry in this region using local clay.

Today there is a superb museum at nearby Jackfield where not only do they have many more examples of the tile maker's art but also have a number of entire rooms that have been moved into the museum so that you can see how these tiles were intended to look when they were used. Tiles from here were sent all over the world – they can even be found in Moscow's underground system.

At the next junction turn left into Legges Hill which takes its name from the Legg family. They were clay pipe producers who, incidentally, were already producing clay products even before tobacco had been introduced into Britain. The building on the left of the street is a former school that was opened in 1892.

Standing on this steep hillside there's an excellent view of the valley ahead, with houses spread all around. Until the 1600s Broseley was just a sleepy little hamlet with few inhabitants. That century, however, saw the development of coal mining in this area and suddenly there was an influx of people coming in to work the mines. Until then this area of land had been an open common but those new people needed somewhere to live and they started building their shacks all over this open, common land. In fact there were so many new houses built here that the local people, despairing at the loss of their grazing land, on one occasion rioted and burnt down the new buildings. But, as you can see, the newcomers were here to stay, rebuilding their shacks wherever they thought they could get away with it, often with nothing more than narrow little alleyways leading to them. This total lack of proper planning in the layout means that today this part of Broseley is one of the most fascinating parts of the modern town.

Many of the early narrow alleyways survived to become present-day rights of way and, in Broseley, they are known as *jitties*. It's worth exploring as many of the jitties as you can but, for now, we will only see two. First of all turn right into Simpson's Lane. The first jitty you see is on the left. It's called Ding Dong Steps, supposedly because of the sound made by the metal studs in the clogs of people who used to walk along it. Then a little further on, on the right, is Lloyds Jitty and this is the jitty the tour follows.

From Lloyds Jitty you emerge onto Quarry Road and, bearing right, come out once more on King Street. Walk back along King Street, passing the old, tiled butcher's shop and, this time, keep straight on so that you are walking behind the back of the pipe museum. Reaching the junction with Queen Street, the house just beyond the turning is the delightfully named Burnt House, so-called because there was a fire here in 1883 which partly destroyed it.

Continue along the road (now known as Cape Street) until you reach the High Street once more. Turn left and walk towards the centre of the town, stopping when you reach a pub with a wonderful iron sign, The Ironmaster, reminding us of all the local ironmasters of the past but particularly, I hope, John "Ironmad" Wilkinson.

We know today that Abraham Darby kicked off what has become known as the Industrial Revolution when, in Coalbrookdale in 1709, he pioneered a method of smelting iron ore using coke rather than the much more wasteful charcoal. Consequently many people today tend to think of Coalbrookdale as the place where everything started, forgetting the

many inventions made in other towns all around this area and by other men such as Wilkinson. It's worth finishing this tour, therefore, by reminding ourselves that it was in and around Broseley that the first iron rails were made, the first iron wheels were made, the first iron boat was built. This town has a heritage to be proud of.

As you walk through Broseley notice all the multicoloured bricks, often with numerous stripes, used in so many of the buildings all around the town. These are the result of tiles being laid against them in the firing kilns. Presumably they were used here because they weren't considered good enough for fine houses elsewhere but I think they are quite lovely.

Church Stretton

When you find the element *stret*, *strat* or *street* in a town's name it generally means that the settlement was originally positioned astride a Roman road. However, when you then start to look at exactly where the old Roman road ran and study the site of the earliest, usually Saxon, settlement you invariably find that the people lived a little distance from the road. This is exactly the case with the Strettons.

The line of the old Roman road can still be followed along the streets to the east of the main A49 that are known to this day as Watling Street South and Watling Street North. However the church, where we start this tour and where the early Saxons settled, is some several hundred yards to the west. This often confuses people, but try to imagine yourself as a Saxon settler with your family and a few cows and pigs looking for somewhere to set up home. The old Roman road is certainly useful, indeed you used it to make your way here and it will prove to be useful in the future when you want to encourage people to come here to trade. But, in the meantime, it will also serve as an easy route for other invaders or potential trouble makers of all kinds. And so, when choosing just where to live, you select a spot that's convenient to the road but not too close – it's safer to build your house somewhere hidden amongst the trees.

Which is why the Strettons, the "settlements on the street", weren't really on the street at all, at least not for many hundreds of years.

So our tour of Church Stretton starts in the churchyard of St Laurence's Church, in the heart of the area where, in all probability the early Saxons lived and where, once they had converted to Christianity, they built their church. Not that anything remains of that church today. The earliest part of the church is the nave dating back to Norman times, while the tower was added in the 13th century.

Before you leave the churchyard, see if you can find Ann Cook's grave with its unusual inscription. Partially eroded you can still make out bits of it. Originally it read as follows:

> *On a Thursday was born*
> *On a Thursday made a bride*
> *On a Thurday broke her leg*
> *And on a Thursday died*

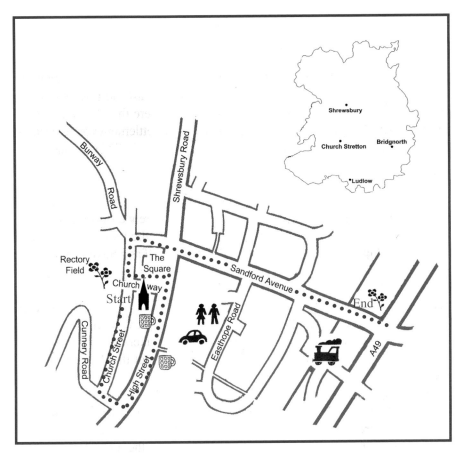

There's a delightful story about how there came to be three separate settlements all called Stretton sitting alongside each other. The king (and stories differ as to just which king it was) was visiting the area and first of all he visited the settlement to the south. "Oh, this is a pleasant little town," he remarked and so the settlement came to be known as Little Stretton. Then he came here and "What a magnificent church you have", he said and so this place came to be known as Church Stretton. Finally the king visited the settlement a short distance to the north and this time he said, "Oh, but they're all called Stretton" so that it came to be known as All Stretton. How much credence you put in this story I leave to you.

But St Laurence's Church is certainly a fine one. When you visit it, seek out the window (in the south transcept) dedicated to Hesba Stretton. To learn more about her you will need to go on the Wellington walk.

Leave the churchyard by the gate facing the main door and turn left to walk down Church Street. Stop when you reach the junction with Cunnery Road. (If you're feeling particularly strenuous you may care to explore on your own by turning right and walking up to the Long Mynd Hotel. It's a very steep climb but the view from the hotel overlooking the valley is superb.)

Turn left in Cunnery Road and make your way to the High Street where you turn left once again. Notice the black and white house across the street opposite the corner. It's known as Tudor Cottage and is thought to be one of the oldest buildings in the town. Church Stretton suffered a serious fire in 1593 so that nearly all the timber buildings in the town date from the rebuilding that followed.

Walking up High Street there's a hall on the left called the Silvester Horne Institute. Charles Silvester Horne was a Congregationalist minister here who also served as a Liberal MP for Ipswich. He liked to claim that he was the first Member of Parliament in full pastoral charge of a Congregational church since the 1650s. Horne died in 1914.

Further along the street, on the right, is the King's Arms pub. Like the Tudor Cottage this, too, dates from the period of rebuilding that followed the 1593 fire. You need to walk to the end of the pub and look back at it in order to see it properly, because from here it is possible to see that this, too, is timber-framed.

In fact, a number of the buildings in the town are, despite outward appearances, timber-framed structures. Some are now covered with stucco, others with brick facades. It's always worth looking carefully at the roof lines and gable ends to see if you can spot them. Further along the street, however, there is a delightful timber house which has recently been restored, the Old Barn. This gets its name because it probably once served as a barn for the next pub on our route – the Buck's Head.

Originally a large farmhouse on what would have been the most important position in town, right next to the church, the Buck's Head has timbers in it that pre-date the 1593 fire – some go back to 1296. However, most of the building dates to the rebuilding period that followed the fire so, if not totally destroyed by the fire, certainly it was considerably damaged by it. Incidentally, the plaque over the entrance indicates later work.

Continue along High Street until you come to an open area, The Square. The earliest charter giving the townspeople permission to hold a regular market was granted by King John in 1214. In those days the market was held on a Wednesday but it was changed by Edward III, in 1337, to Thursday and that's the day on which the town's market is still held. As with other towns around the country several markets and fairs developed over the years. One of Church Stretton's annual markets was held every November; it drew people from far and wide but it came to be known as the Dead Man's Fair. This sounds horrendous and, indeed, it is. The nickname came about because many people coming to trade at this fair would travel across the hills of the Long Mynd. Occasionally the weather at that time of year could be treacherous and it wasn't unknown for people to die while trying to cross the hills when travelling to, or from, the fair.

These hills can still be dangerous. When the mists descend it can be impossible for even local people to know exactly where they are and they become lost or disorientated. The Revd Donald Carr, however, was lucky because he survived a storm in the hills in the 1860s and wrote a book describing his ordeal, *A Night in the Snow*. Carr was a vicar with parishes on both sides of the Long Mynd and would regularly walk on a Sunday between the two parishes to conduct services. One Sunday he left his parish at Ratlinghope to walk across the hills just as snow was beginning to fall. Unaware of the ferocity of the approaching storm Carr decided he could easily return home but, as he walked across the hills, he lost his bearings and ended up suffering from snow blindness and completely unaware of where he was. He was fortunate to be found the following morning before he died.

There are a variety of building types just around the Square – timber-framed structures (some partially covered), brick buildings and, across the road, the wonderful Victorian façade of H Salt & Co.

Leave the Square by the Churchway – it starts from the south-western corner of the Square leading, appropriately, to the Church. Opposite the end of Churchway is the entrance to Rectory Field with the Rectory Wood beyond. So called because it was once land belonging to the church, the wood is now open to the public and has a nature trail in it. It was the Revd John Mainwaring who, in the late 1700s, arranged the original planting of the woodland here and it is understood that he was a friend of the famous landscaper, Capability Brown, who may well have advised him. This is a lovely area in which to walk at any time of year but it's particularly pretty in late winter when the snowdrops are in flower.

If you don't wish to explore the wood then, when you reach Church Street, turn to your right. The street widens and you will soon see ahead of you Burway Road leading up the hill to the left. This would have been the road across the hills used by those people travelling to and from the Dead Man's Fair.

The road is still treacherous, primarily for car drivers. It should not be used by those of a nervous disposition since, around every bend, drivers are likely to find idling sheep who feel that the road is very much their own territory.

It was the hills and the steep tracks into it that gave Church Stretton its nickname of *Little Switzerland*. Some people will tell you that the nickname was also apt because all the services in the town ran like clockwork – I'd love to know if the present population agrees. To this day Church Stretton is very popular with people coming to the area when they retire. This tradition began in Victorian times – apparently Victorian gentlemen and their wives who had served in India and enjoyed brief holidays in the hills came here in their droves because they thought the town was very "similar to Simla".

Walk uphill along Burway Road just as far as the first cottage on the left – Pryll Cottage. Another timber-framed building with a brick skin it sits over the Townbrook, the stream that brought water down from the hill to the settlement. Once the stream ran all the way through the town but these

34

days it has been culverted and runs underground to reappear near the railway station.

Across the road, the benches make this a pleasant place to sit and watch the world go by. On the hill above stands Church Stretton's war memorial.

From here walk down Burway Road to the junction with High Street and Shrewsbury Road. Once again there are a number of attractive houses, particularly those on the left hand side of the road. The antiques shop that sits beside the road junction was once the town's post office.

Pause when you get to the junction to look at the building opposite, on the left of Sandford Avenue. Now a conglomeration of shops it was once the Sandford Hotel and, when opened in the 1860s, it served visitors coming on the train for holidays walking in the hills. It has quite an interesting mishmash of styles and includes within it a 16th century malthouse (remembered in the name of the pub on the left). Sadly the hotel closed following a fire in 1968 in which five people died and the building was then divided into the many units that you now see.

Cross the road and walk down Sandford Avenue. This is the main shopping area of present-day Church Stretton. Many of the shop buildings here date from Victorian times, a result of the increased commercial importance of the road following the opening of the railway station.

Walking down Sandford Avenue look out for No 22, on the right. The clock on the building was first put up because the shop then was used by a watchmaker. For years, however, it didn't work, but has now been restored.

St Dunstan's

During the Second World War the Long Mynd Hotel was taken over as a hospital by St Dunstan's. St Dunstan's was founded in 1915 for those who had been blinded in combat during World War One and an important part of its work is the rehabilitation of those who have lost their sight.

The hotel wasn't the only building in the town taken over by St Dunstan's – many private houses were used too. In order to encourage the men and women who came here to find their way around the town a system of ropes was set up. These ropes were of different thicknesses according to where in the town they went, so that individuals could get around the town independently.

Further along the street there is a large building, just beyond the junction with Easthope Road, that now houses an antiques market. Originally another malthouse, this building has had many uses over the years. During the Second World War it served as a canteen for troops based in the area. It was also one of the many buildings in the town used by St Dunstan's – when it was used as a workshop to train for new trades those people blinded in the war.

Walk on until you reach the bridge over the railway. This is a main line linking Shrewsbury and Ludlow and today the station that serves the town is to the south of the bridge but, originally, it was on the northern side – you can still see the old station building beside the line.

Having crossed over the bridge, on your left is the town's park where our tour ends, another pleasant spot to sit down for a rest despite the noise of the traffic on the busy main road, the A49, just beyond. One final story, before we finish - many people will tell you that the road marks the line of the old Roman road through the Stretton Gap. This is not so. The line of the street that gave the Strettons their name is the road beyond that lies parallel to the A49. Once that early Saxon settlement had developed and travelling along roads became relatively safe people abandoned the Roman road and started to use the road that now forms the High Street in the town. This, inevitably, became snarled up with traffic so that, in the 1930s a new bypass was built, the road you see ahead of you. The new road had no sooner been built than the Second World War broke out and so, for much of the war, the new road was closed to civilian traffic and instead was used as a car park for military vehicles, particularly in the months leading up to D-Day.

Baron Leighton of Stretton in the County of Salop
Frederic Leighton was a painter and sculptor born in Scarborough in 1830. Linked to the Pre-Raphaelite movement in art, his paintings are mainly biblical or classical in subject matter. In the New Years Honours List of 1896 he was created Baron Leighton of Stretton, the first painter ever to be given a peerage. Sadly, he died the day after he received the honour and, as he was unmarried and had no heirs, the title died with him. His was therefore the shortest-lived title in the English peerage.

Clun

Clun is the most delightful little town, nestling in the valley where it guards a bridging point across the River Clun. We are in the hills of southern Shropshire here and so, be warned, this walk has one or two steep sections. It starts where the first settlement started – at the church.

It seems strange to find the church on what is obviously the edge of the settlement but this is because the focus of the town moved in Norman times. The first settlers established their homes here, close enough to the river that they could control who crossed it but high enough on the hill that they could also see who might be coming their way.

We have no idea when those first people arrived but the name *Clun* gives a small clue – it's of Celtic origin and must predate the arrival of the Anglo-Saxons in Britain. One school of thought as to its meaning suggests that the name is an early form of the modern *llan* that appears in many Welsh placenames, and in these cases it always refers to an early Christian site of some sort – a church or a preaching site or perhaps just a place associated with an early saint. So, standing in the churchyard, we are probably standing in a place that has had religious significance for over fifteen hundred years and, perhaps, for even longer, going back to pagan times. But we'll never know for sure.

Looking at the church the first thing that strikes you is its sturdiness and the solidity of its tower. It may be a religious building but it has a certain military aspect to it and this was deliberate. Shropshire, being a border county, was subject to constant attack by the Welsh and a thriving town, such as Clun once was, would have been a most attractive target for such attacks. This tower therefore served both as a lookout-post and a place of refuge.

Do take the opportunity to explore the church while you are here. Dedicated to St George, parts of it date back to Norman times – one of the first things you notice on entering the church are the solid Norman columns along

The grave is that of the playwright, John Osborne, who died in 1994. His play Look Back in Anger, *first performed in 1956, took the theatrical world by storm. Osborne's former home, The Hurst, lies just outside Clun and is now used as a training centre for writers. The inscription on the tombstone comes from another of his works,* The Entertainer. *His wife lies beside him – look out for the delightful inscription on her tombstone, too.*

37

the aisle of the nave. However several hundred years of wear and tear meant that the church needed to be heavily restored in the 1870s. Fortunately, one result of this restoration was the revealing of the 14th century roof timbers over the north aisle.

Having explored the church, start the tour by walking through the lychgate and down towards the river. Today this is very much a residential street but once all the houses were owned by artisans who carried out their trades from their homes. There would have been cobblers, tailors, weavers and at least four pubs along here.

Stop when you reach the bottom of the street, beside the red-brick building next to the bridge. This building dates from 1870 when it was a meeting place for the Clun Temperance Society. With at least four pubs along Church Street and numerous others on the far side of the river, it's not difficult to see that there may once have been a need for a temperance society. When built, the trustees of the building signed a contract agreeing that intoxicating liquor would never be sold from the premises – I wonder if that is still part of the deeds.

Before continuing the tour by crossing over the bridge into the town, first of all take a detour into the car park from where you can see the bridge properly. This sturdy little bridge dates back to the 14th century and was built as a packhorse bridge. It was never intended for the kind of traffic that uses it nowadays and it can sometimes be dangerously busy. This also means that the parapets on the bridge suffer from constant knocks by passing vehicles.

Before you leave the car park look to the right of the toilet block at the far side and you will see another bridge, this time a wooden footbridge. Andrew Lloyd Webber, the composer, was on a cycling holiday in the area some years ago during which time he visited Clun. That bridge was built using money he raised so that people could cross easily to the castle site beyond. Our route to the castle, however, takes us through the town so you now need to take your life in your hands and return to the road in order to cross over the stone bridge. There are passing points on the bridge where you can take refuge if vehicles do come along – it's said that "twill sharpen your wits to cross Clun bridge".

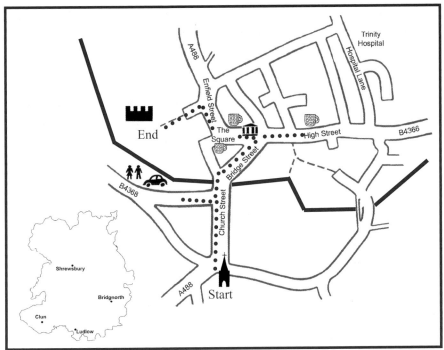

If you should visit Clun during the first weekend in May you may well find the bridge crowded not with vehicles but with people in strange costumes. This is when the town holds its annual Green Man Festival. Green Men feature on both Christian and pagan carvings (and pub signs) throughout England. Normally carvings depict just a head with what appears to be greenery growing all around. Where and when they originated and exactly what they mean no-one knows. One thing we can be sure of is that they are associated with fertility and springtime. Here in Clun the Green Man Festival lasts three days culminating in the *Battle of the Bridge* when the Queen of Cold challenges the Green Man. If the Green Man should lose the battle then summer will not come to the Clun valley that year!

Once you have crossed the bridge follow the main road, Bridge Street, bearing right. As you go look out for Creswell House on the right. It was the home of Bruce Bairnsfather in 1941. Born in India in 1888, Bairnsfather had served on the Western Front during the First World War. Suffering in hospital from shellshock, he was commissioned to do weekly drawings for a magazine and he developed a cartoon character named *Old Bill*. Later, in the 1920s and 1930s, several plays and films were produced using Old Bill and, in the Second World War, Bairnsfather was appointed as an official cartoonist for the American Forces in Europe.

At the road junction bear right once more and walk a little way along the High Street, stopping opposite the old 16th century Sun inn. In his collection of poems, *A Shropshire Lad*, published in the 1890s, AE Housman describes the villages along the Clun valley as being "the quietest under the sun". Local tradition has it that in his original version of the poem Housman used the word "drunkenest". Perhaps that explains why, towards the end of the street, there was once yet more evidence of the need for a Temperance Society locally with a Temperance Hotel.

Today many of the old buildings that line this street are private homes although once they would have been shops and workshops (and pubs).

Now retrace your steps and walk to The Square. Medieval castles, such as the one we will see shortly, seldom stood entirely alone. Lords in their castles needed constant supplies of money and a ready source would have been the local people. As happened in Ludlow, Bridgnorth and elsewhere in Shropshire, once the castle was built a market was soon established where local people were forced to trade and then pay tolls for the privilege. Here, of course, there was already a settlement but, prior to the building of the castle, it would have been focussed on the church on the other side of the river. With the building of the castle the town's heart moved here.

Entering the Square, the first building on your right is the Town Hall. It was built by Edward Clive, son of the famous Robert Clive, Clive of India. Notice the coat of arms over the door facing the Square, the arms of the Earls of Powis. Edward Clive married the daughter of the Earl of Powis hence the presence of an Indian elephant on the modern coat of arms of the family. Incidentally, you may have thought as you followed the walk that Clun is very small for a town and should perhaps be defined as a village instead. Don't dare make such comments to local people – they are very proud to call Clun a town. Indeed Clun received its first charter to be a town in the 14th century and the fact that it has a Town Hall confirms its status.

Today the Town Hall is used as a museum and, if it is open, you must take the opportunity to look inside. As you would expect it houses exhibits associated with local history but it also has visiting exhibitions and demonstrations on occasion.

The medieval market would have taken up much more space than you see here now, covering the land between here and the castle itself. Surrounding that market, just as today, you would once have had numerous shops and pubs. One interesting building facing onto the Square is the Buffalo Inn at the far end – it is best known for its association with the writer Sir Walter Scott who stayed there in 1825. It's said that he used Clun's castle, which we visit next, as the inspiration for his Garde Doleureuse in his book *The Betrothed*, a story set in the Welsh borderlands at the time of the Crusades.

Cross the Square and leave along the main road to the right – Enfield Street – just beyond the White Horse pub. Look out for the footpath sign directing you to the left to the castle (take care to avoid the road, marked *Private* that you see first – it may look as though it goes to the castle but it doesn't). Stop when you find yourself standing with the bowling green on your right.

The ruined castle sits on an imposing site watching over the Clun valley and looking towards the hills of Wales to the west. The Welsh borders, or *Marches*, were lined with a series of castles all the way from Chester to Chepstow, built to protect England from incursions by the Welsh and the first castle here was part of that line of military fortifications. It was built around 1090 by Picot de Say, the Norman who had been given these lands.

De Say's castle was a typical motte-and-bailey lay-out and here the form of such castles is clear. Ahead, dominated by the surviving ruins, you see the motte – a man-made mound rising above the rest of the castle site where the keep, the final stronghold, was built. Notice how, around the motte, there is a well-defined moat which gave the motte additional defence, should the castle be attacked and the rest of it forced to surrender. The bailey was the service part of the castle and it is the area to the left, where the hilltop

has clearly been flattened. Within the castle walls here would have been the stables, armouries, workshops and living quarters for the ordinary soldiers. Clun's castle is also interesting because it had a second bailey – the area on your right that serves as a bowling green. This was once the site of the town's courthouse – it was pulled down in 1780 and the stone was used to build the Town Hall that you saw in the Square.

De Say's original castle was built of wood. It was replaced with a stone castle around the turn of the 12th and 13th centuries. We know the castle was besieged by the Welsh in 1196 when it was reduced to "ashes" and perhaps this implies that the original wooden castle was still in use at that time. It was again captured in 1214 but when Llewelyn the Great tried to take it yet again in 1234 he was unable to do so and vented his frustration by burning the town instead. The end of the 1200s saw Wales come largely under the control of King Edward I and from then on the castle ceased to be militarily important.

Instead it came to be associated with pleasure. It may not look like it today, but here you are in the middle of the Clun Forest. In medieval times forests were not necessarily totally wooded areas as we think today, instead the term meant an area used by the local nobility for hunting, an area under "forest law" where deer were protected and woebetide the peasant who tried to poach. So local lords came to use this castle as a rather grand hunting lodge – King Edward III once came here to enjoy the hunting.

While the men are out hunting the ladies want to enjoy the place too – and so, a *pleasuance* was developed. This consisted of formal gardens, pavilions, even fish ponds, that were laid out in the area below the castle, between it and the river beyond.

The tour ends here but please explore the castle ruins before you leave. It is possible to walk around them and then return to the car park by the river over the wooden bridge – there's a track down to the left.

Did you know that the word hospital, *meaning a place where the sick are cared for, comes from the same root as the word* hospitality? *In other words, early hospitals were often places that not only cared for the sick but also tended those people unable to care for themselves for other reasons too so that, today, many almshouses around the country have "hospital" in their name.*

Trinity Hospital is an example – founded in 1614, it provided accommodation for twelve "old men of good character" who were expected to wear a uniform consisting of a blue gown with a red and silver badge emblazoned upon it. Top hats had to be worn when they went out on a Sunday.

In the garden of Trinity Hospital is a delightful sculpture showing two old men of Trinity in their uniforms that you should try to see. You are welcome to enter the courtyard garden but do please bear in mind that this is a private garden for the residents who live here. Incidentally, the rules have recently been changed so you may well see ladies who live here now too.

Ellesmere

The tour of Ellesmere starts beside St Mary's Church which sits between the heart of the present town and the mere.

Although there has been a church on this site since Saxon times, the present one is largely Victorian. Some older parts are still visible inside – the chapels that sit either side of the chancel, for example. To my mind, however, one of the most fascinating survivals in this church is the tombstone of a scrivener. It dates from the 14th century and is in remarkably good condition – probably because when it was found it had been turned upside down and reused so that the original underside was the side that was weathered. A scrivener was a professional writer and, if you look carefully, you can see his pouch where he kept his writing equipment hanging from his belt.

To understand Ellesmere's history requires a walk up to the site of the Norman castle. The climb is quite steep and there are steps at the top so you may wish to forgo this loop but, if you can include it, the views from the top make the climb worthwhile. Walk up Church Hill and at the road junction go through the metal gate on the left into the parking area of

Once upon a time, so the story goes, there was an old woman who lived in the valley below. That old woman had a well in her garden which supplied her with fresh water. One year there was a drought and all the local wells in the district dried up – except for this one. The old woman's neighbours came to her to ask if they could take water from her well but she refused. The spirit of the well, hearing the old woman's refusal, was appalled and decided to teach her a lesson. That spirit then caused the water in the well to rise and rise and rise, until eventually the old woman was drowned and not just her house but the valley too was covered in water.

Ellesmere's Bowling Club. Follow the road as far up the hill as you can, climb the steps at the top and you are beside the clubhouse. There's a paved path to the right, beside the clubhouse, so that you don't need to walk over the green in order to admire the fine view over the town and towards Wales. What a site for a castle!

Go just beyond the clubhouse and look right so that you can see the Mere that gives Ellesmere its name – "the lake belonging to someone called Elli". The lake is a survival from the last Ice Age when meltwater became trapped here. It once covered a much larger area than it does today, filling the low lying land to the west and south of the castle as well, so that the land where you are standing was once a promontory surrounded by water on three sides. This natural moat meant that this was an excellent defensive position and the first people to take advantage of this site were our ancient Iron Age

45

ancestors who built a hill fort here – so that Ellesmere can claim to be one of the oldest continuously inhabited settlement sites in the country.

It was a Norman lord called William Peveril who built the castle in 1120. Some years later, however, he was found guilty of poisoning the Earl of Chester and lost his lands. Coming under royal control the castle was subsequently part of the dowry of King John's illegitimate daughter, Joan, when she was married off to Llewelyn the Great in 1205. This was definitely not a love match – the king was trying to gain greater control over Llewelyn who had been forced to swear allegiance to him. While he held Ellesmere, Llewelyn gave it its first charter in 1216 and the rights to hold a market. By 1230 the town was once again in English hands. With the conquest of the Welsh under Edward I later that same century, the castle ceased to be militarily important. From then on it declined so that by the mid 1500s it had all but disappeared.

Incidentally, before you leave you may be interested to know that Ellesmere has another claim to longevity – the bowling green is said to be one of the oldest in the country, having been in use for over 350 years.

Retrace your steps to the gate and cross Church Hill into St John's Hill. You may notice in the ground on the right a strange pattern of rectangular stones forming a kind of crazy paving just in front of a garage. Believe it or not this is an anti-tank defence surviving from the Second World War. The concrete blocks fill former holes into which barriers could be inserted in order to block access.

Walking down St John's Hill you are walking through the old medieval town of Ellesmere, below the castle but above the water level of the mere. Although many of the buildings here appear to date from around the 18th century, many have timber-framed cores that are much older.

Turn into the first road on your right – The Mount. It may look like a private drive but it isn't. Walk to the end, bearing right where there is a footpath through a gate to bring you back to the church.

This time walk around the church to the left so that you have a glimpse of the Mere. If you get the chance later to walk around the lake you will discover that much of the area has been laid out with gardens. At one time these gardens were the site of a tannery – with all the effluent from the leather working flowing into the lake one doesn't dare think of what the

Pinfold Lane was where once there was a pinfold (or pound) where stray animals would have been kept. Such strays were reclaimed on payment of a fine.

quality of the water that the local people were drinking must have been like. The first gardens were laid out in the early 19th century when the land was bought by the then Earl of Bridgwater who lived in Ellesmere House (the building just across the road on your right, now a residential home). Apparently, when the Earl wasn't in residence the grounds of the house were opened for the "better sort of people" within the town to use. In 1953 the gardens were presented to

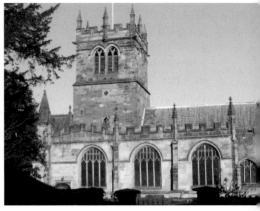

the town by Lord Brownlow. They are known as the Cremorne Gardens because the family also once owned estates in Cremorne in Italy.

Across the main road, No 25 Church Street housed offices for the Brownlow Estate. The offices included a flat and Evelyn Waugh stayed here in 1936 while writing *Waugh in Abyssinia*. It's also said that the Prince of Wales (the future Duke of Windsor) once stayed here.

Notice how high above the road you are. In fact this road, the present main road to Shrewsbury, dates from the 1800s and was built after the water levels had been lowered all around the mere and the town. When the road was originally built the intention was that the ground from the church should slope gently down to it but instead it soon became apparent that the removal of the soil here had badly affected the foundations of the church and so the wall below had to be built to stabilise the area.

Leave the churchyard through the gate onto Church Street, bearing left. Almost immediately on the left is the Red Lion, parts of which date from the 16th century. When first built, the inn sat on the edge of the town, above the lake, with a market place beside it. All the houses on the far side of the street date from the 19th century after the surrounding land had been drained and the focus of the town moved west. By this time the Red Lion had become a coaching inn serving stagecoach services that ran to Chester and Wrexham.

Walk past the Red Lion and turn left when you reach Watergate Street, just past the Victorian letter box. The curving line of this street gives a clue to the fact that in medieval times it followed the shoreline of the mere, so this would then have been the western boundary of Ellesmere. Being near the water and away from the better houses around the castle it was also where much of the town's early industry took place.

At the end of Watergate Street the road junction is dominated by the Ellesmere Hotel, another former coaching inn. This inn, however, had an interesting connection with the nearby canal. When plans to build the Ellesmere Canal (as it was first known) were made, money needed to be raised and so shares were sold to a public only too keen to buy (canal shares in the latter 1700s were the equivalent "must-buy" to railway shares in the 1800s). The shares went on sale here on 10 September 1792 and in that one day around one million pounds was raised – an incredible sum of money for the time. Incidentally, the hotel wasn't known as the Ellesmere Hotel at the time, it was then called the Royal Oak; it has also been known as the Bridgwater Arms.

At the crossroads beside the Ellesmere Hotel, walk ahead into Birch Road until you reach another inn, the White Hart. It dates from the 16th century and is said to be the oldest pub in Shropshire. It isn't, but it's certainly the oldest one in Ellesmere. Notice the pun on its name in the form of a white heart marked out in the cobbles on the ground in front of the main entrance.

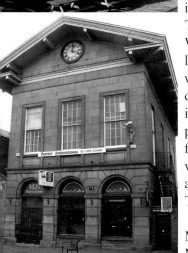

Return to the Ellesmere Hotel and turn left into the High Street. At the far end is an open area, The Square, overlooked by the former Town Hall. We are standing now on what was once, if not a lake, certainly very boggy ground and it's said that when the Town Hall was built in 1830 piles had to be driven 30 feet into the ground below in order to give it steady foundations. Somehow, amongst all those piles, space was made for a sizeable cellar. When first built the ground floor served as an open market while upstairs there was a large assembly room. For a time it served as a museum and then a cinema. Today it sits vacant.

Cross the Square and make your way up Market Street beyond. It was once called Swine Market Street. Look out for the White Lion on the right – dating from 1550 it is now an antique shop although it was once a pub. At the top of Market Street, on the left, is the entrance to the old Rennet Works. Rennet comes from the stomach lining of cattle and is used to coagulate milk for cheese-making – an essential ingredient in this Cheshire cheese producing part of the world. Indeed, at one time most of the rennet used for cheese-making throughout England came from here.

Turn left in Victoria Street and then left again at the bottom of the hill into Scotland Street. Overlooking the road junction is Tudor Cottage, one of several cottages hereabouts that have been recently restored with help from the Shropshire Buildings Preservation Trust.

Then walk as far as the entrance to Wharf Road, on your right. Opposite the road stands the Black Lion Hotel, yet another pub that is a timber-framed building hidden behind a later brick façade.

Wharf Road is an odd name for a street in the middle of the country but it does indeed lead to a wharf – serving the Ellesmere Canal (or the Shropshire Union Canal as it is known today). When it was built the Ellesmere Canal was intended to complete a canal network linking the Dee and Severn Rivers with the Trent and also the Mersey estuary – hence the name of Ellesmere Port to the north. It was one of the last canal systems to be built and, before it was completed, the new railway system had begun to be developed so that the Ellesmere Canal was never finished.

When you reach the canal basin stop near to the old crane and look around you. As I write this, the whole area is undergoing redevelopment and soon it will be very difficult to imagine how this area once looked. Some of the oldest buildings are those behind you – which include a delightful row of terrace houses, built as homes for employees on the Bridgwater Estate.

To the right of the canal was where once the town's gas works were based. Here, too, until the late 1980s was the Ellesmere Creamery. The Creamery was established in 1917, during the First World War, to supply milk to London – the milk was collected from farms in the region and cooled here using water from the canal before being sent on by rail.

Looking towards the canal, the gable end of the warehouse on the left reads "Shropshire Union Railways and Canal Company" – a reminder that the Ellesmere Canal was incorporated into one of the railway companies; this happened as early as 1846. Goods of all sorts besides cheese and milk came through here – timber, roof slates, farm equipment even passengers travelling to and from Wales.

Our tour of Ellesmere ends at the canal basin but you may wish to

walk along the towpath to the canal junction ahead of you. The fine building, with its curved windows, that overlooks the junction was the headquarters of the Ellesmere Canal Company and also provided accommodation for the Resident Engineer and Account Agent. Beech House, as it is known, is now private. Buildings beside it, however, are still used for the canal – there are workshops for the maintenance of narrowboats using the canals and even one building with a dry dock.

SCOTLAND STREET

This always strikes me as a most odd name for a town in England, particularly since it goes west in the direction of Wales rather than Scotland. In fact it comes from the word scot *or* sceot *and originally referred to a local tax on land. It's a word that has a Scandinavian origin and once, to describe something as "scot free" meant that it was free of this particular form of tax although we tend today to use the term to mean that someone has avoided payment altogether.*

Ironbridge

The tour of Ironbridge begins on the bridge itself. Do be aware, however, that to explore Ironbridge properly requires walking up and down many steep slopes and flights of stairs.

To start, make your way to the centre of the Iron Bridge and stand so that you are looking upstream. An understanding of Ironbridge, and of the part played by this entire area in bringing about what we now term the *Industrial Revolution*, cannot proceed without a brief look at the natural and geological features of the area.

Looking upstream you can see the line of the river wending its way through hills that climb steeply on either side. This is the Ironbridge Gorge and it was created some 15,000 years ago at the end of the last Ice Age. As ice melted it formed a huge lake to the west. Water from that lake overflowed and it was this overflow that carved out the valley through which the River Severn still flows today. However, because the water is being pushed through such a narrow gorge the currents move rapidly and so, from early times, this fast-moving river would have been ideal to power water mills.

But it wasn't just water power. In the hills around us there was also a rich supply of coal, iron-ore and limestone. You can see, too, that the hills, despite modern developments, are still covered with trees – this provided charcoal, then an essential ingredient in the production of iron. There was clay here, too, suitable for producing pottery and tiles. So it was that there had been industry here long before the Industrial Revolution began.

Then, in the early 1700s, Abraham Darby arrived. An ironmaster, originally from Dudley, Darby bought a furnace at nearby Coalbrookdale. He was looking for a method by which he could smelt iron-ore using coke rather than charcoal. It seems strange to us these days, but using coke from coal rather than charcoal from wood, would then have been seen as a much "greener" option since trees would not need to be constantly felled and left to re-grow in order to keep producing charcoal.

Bedlam Furnace
This massive brick structure, on Waterloo Street, is all that remains today of one of the earliest furnaces in the area to use coke to smelt iron-ore. Now a protected ancient monument, it once consisted of two furnaces and an engine room with bellows. There was also a brickyard just behind the site.

The smelting of iron-ore with coke had other advantages too, the main one being that far greater quantities of iron could be produced than ever before. Within a few years the whole valley was lined with furnaces all spewing out their black smoke and what must have been a very pretty valley (much like today) was changed into "an idea of the heathen Hell".

If you get the chance while you are here do try to visit the Museum of Iron in Coalbrookdale. Here the story of iron production through the ages is explained and the furnace that Abraham Darby used for his experiments can still be seen. It was last used around 1818, and then became engulfed in later foundry works and forgotten. Subsequently rediscovered in 1959, it had to be totally unearthed – real industrial archaeology.

We'll take a closer look at the bridge itself later but, for now, walk to the south and stop outside the tollhouse. You may have seen the date 1779 painted on the centre of the bridge. That was the date the bridge was erected but it didn't actually open to the public until 1 January 1881. This delay was due to the time required to build the necessary roads, especially the steep Bridge Bank leading down the hill from Broseley.

Do take time to read the list of tolls. Notice that it states that even the Royal Family has to pay to cross over. When it opened the original charge for pedestrians was a halfpenny but it was possible for regular users to buy season tickets and one guinea (£1.05) bought you an annual pass. There was only one man who was allowed to cross over for free and that was the ferryman who previously had rowed people across the river at this point and had been put out of business when the bridge was built.

Retrace your steps to walk across the bridge to the northern side, the sunny side. There's a local saying that, although the northern bank of the river may be the "sunny side" it's the southern bank that was the "money side" since it was on that side that the tollhouse stood.

Facing the bridge is the Tontine Hotel. Once the bridge was built it immediately attracted visitors from all around the world and this hotel was built in 1883 to accommodate them. It's name is unusual and derives from the name of an Italian banker, Lorenzo de Tonti, who developed the tontine form of investment in 1653. Such an investment is one in which there are several investors, each of whom

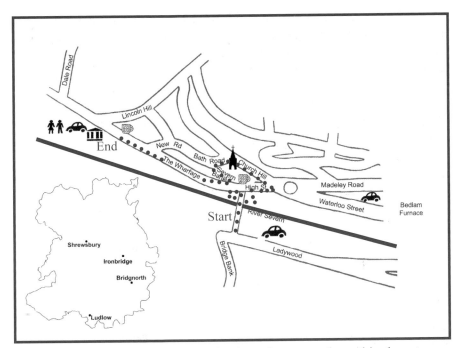

earns his dividends from it while alive but who cannot leave his share to any individual heirs. Instead, as investors die, their holdings are passed on to the surviving investors. This ensures that the business ends up in the hands of one person rather than being split amongst many heirs.

Don't cross the road but, instead, turn left and make your way under the bridge. Stop before you get too close. Now, for the first time, you can see the Iron Bridge it all its glory. Today, and with good reason, it is used as the symbol for not just the Industrial Revolution but also for the whole Telford

district of Shropshire. Undoubtedly, when it was planned Abraham Darby (the original Darby's grandson) saw it as a public relations exercise in which he could promote the versatility of the iron he was producing – an extremely expensive public relations exercise as it turned out, but most effective.

The idea for an iron bridge was first suggested in 1773 by the Shrewsbury architect, Thomas Farnolls Pritchard, in a letter to John "Ironmad" Wilkinson.

In 1776, an Act of Parliament was passed allowing the bridge to be built. Pritchard had begun his career as a carpenter and, by this time, was well known throughout Shropshire as an architect of fine buildings. This, however, was his first attempt at designing a bridge made of iron. He died in 1777, the year that work on the bridge commenced, and we have no idea today just how much of its ultimate design was his or to what degree this was modified by Abraham Darby, who actually built it.

Certainly it's easy to see the influence of Pritchard's carpentry background in the design. Look carefully at the way in which the bridge has been constructed. Notice all the joints – dovetail joints, tenon and mortice joints – and the numerous pegs. It's as though a wooden bridge has been built using iron. Have a good look at the bridge and you'll see exactly what I mean.

Now walk under the bridge and climb the steps just beyond, back to the street beside the war memorial. Before the bridge was built there was little more in this area than a few wharfs for the loading and unloading of goods that were to be taken inland to places like Madeley and Wellington. Furthermore, individuals could cross the river at different places depending on where the ferrymen worked. The erection of the bridge changed things totally; from then on everyone who wanted to cross the river was channelled through this same point. Moreover, more and more traders, who previously would have taken their goods to market in towns such as Much Wenlock, started bringing their goods north instead. This total change of focus brought opportunities for the people who lived here and, in next to no time, not only had the Tontine Hotel been built but numerous other services had arrived, necessitating the building of the market square across the road. This was the beginning of the development of the town that we now call Ironbridge.

Don't cross over the road but walk to your right along High Street until you reach a small roundabout. As you walk, take a moment to study the kerbstones on the pavement below you – you'll see that in Ironbridge even the kerbstones are made of iron!

The Ironbridge Rocket

If you are interested in football you may wish to make a little pilgrimage up the hill to Belmont Road. Number 33, Holly Cottage, was the birthplace, in 1924, of Billy Wright who played football for England and Wolverhampton. Nicknamed "the Ironbridge Rocket" he could be described as the first of what is now a common breed – the celebrity football star. He even had a popstar wife (he married one of the Beverley sisters).

Stop at the roundabout. The grey brick building across the road is a former police station and now a restaurant. Notice also the decorative tiles on the façade of the estate agent's shop on the left.

Cross over High Street and take the first turning on the left to climb up Church Hill. Stop when you reach St Luke's Church.

Ironbridge's church only dates from 1836. Until then this area was all part of the parish of Madeley to the north-east. But, as a result of the growth of the population through the 1700s, the need for a new church arose. Unusual in that the church faces the wrong way around with the altar at the west rather than the east end, it is otherwise typical of churches of the period.

The view from the churchyard is spectacular. Notice, particularly, the steep road, Bridge Bank, across the valley and imagine the stagecoaches racing down it before crossing the bridge.

Now walk around the side of St Luke's, leaving the churchyard in Bath Road. Turn left to walk down the hill. Take the first turning left into Severn Bank and keep walking down the steep hill. Although steep, it's an attractive lane with occasional glimpses of the Iron Bridge between the roofs and the chimney pots. Eventually you emerge beside the River Severn once more on the street known as the Wharfage. Cross the road and turn right to walk alongside the river.

The Wharfage, as its name suggests, was once lined with boats delivering and taking on cargo. You can still see the former warehouses with their doors on the upper floors, now often very handsomely converted into houses or offices. The traditional type of boat used to shift goods were *trows*. It's an odd word and is thought to derive from the Saxon word *trog* which meant a trough or hollowed-out vessel. When moving downstream they would go with the current. Coming upstream, however, they needed to be hauled by teams of bowhauliers, foul-mouthed men whose pleasures in life consisted of drinking, womanising, bull-baiting and cock-fighting.

The last working trow on the River Severn ran into the bridge at Bridgnorth in 1895 and promptly sank. However one trow, *The Spry*, has recently been restored and is displayed at the Blists Hill Museum.

As you walk along the Wharfage there are other reminders of the industrial history of the area. Stopping a little before the Swan Inn you will see, across the road, the remains of old limekilns. It was in the Swan, incidentally, that Abraham Darby and his colleagues planned the building of the bridge.

Pause again when you reach the first building on the left. The main entrance is at the other side and it is now a museum, The Museum of the River. However, when built in 1834 it served as a warehouse and you can see in front of you the wharf where the trows were once pulled up to be loaded and unloaded. Later the building became a mineral-water bottling plant and then a garage before being restored as a museum.

While you are here I want you to look at the windows. On the inside there's a marker, about ¾ of the way up, which shows the level to which the water rose in the Great Flood of 1795 – a level well above your head as you stand here. When the Iron Bridge was first erected in 1779 everyone was impressed by it but there were many who didn't quite trust this new technology. That flood was the worst on the Severn in recorded history and it caused many bridges all along the river to be badly damaged, some were totally destroyed. The only bridge to survive unscathed was the Iron Bridge

so that, overnight, a structure that inspired awe and wonder was now also known to be safe.

Our tour ends here. But, in order to really understand just what a busy area Ironbridge once was, you should make the effort to visit this museum, if only to see the model inside of the Ironbridge Gorge as it looked at the time of a royal visit in 1796. It's fascinating to consider what has survived and what has changed over the last 200 years. Studying this model it's easy to understand why the River Severn in the late 18th century was considered the second busiest river in Europe in terms of all the goods being transported along it.

The school at nearby Coalbrookdale was where local writer, Ellis Peters, was educated. She is best known for her Brother Cadfael Chronicles, *stories of a medieval detective monk who lived in 12th century Shrewsbury. Edith Pargeter (her real name) left the school at the age of 14 and went to work as an assistant in a chemist's shop - this turned out to be excellent training for a writer who thereby also learnt about poisons and treatments!*

Ludlow

The tour of Ludlow is a circular route starting from St Lawrence's churchyard and finishing by the main entrance. A town such as Ludlow has much to offer to anyone who cares to take the time to explore it properly and a tour like this cannot do it justice. As with all the others in this book this is intended to encourage you to explore further.

First of all, stand in the churchyard so that you can see the magnificent view to the north. From here you can begin to appreciate what an excellent position Ludlow commands. It's no wonder that the Normans established their castle at the end of the cliff so that they could control movement along the valleys.

For now I want you to turn your back on the view and look at the church instead. The first church here was probably founded in the early 1100s, where the chancel now sits. That first church was soon extended westwards and it's understood that, when this happened, an ancient burial mound was destroyed. At this stage in time we can't be sure of course, but this could imply that perhaps the site had a religious significance in pre-Christian times.

Incidentally, an early word for a Bronze Age burial mound or barrow was a *low* and it is possible, although disputed by many, that this is where the "low" element in the town's name comes from. Perhaps "Lud" was an early chieftain, reputed to be buried in the mound but we'll never know.

That early Norman church was itself extended upwards and outwards so that the building you are looking at now dates largely from the 14th and 15th centuries. St Lawrence's Church is one of the largest parish churches

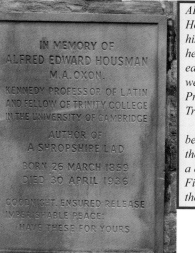

IN MEMORY OF
ALFRED EDWARD HOUSMAN
M.A. OXON.
KENNEDY PROFESSOR OF LATIN
AND FELLOW OF TRINITY COLLEGE
IN THE UNIVERSITY OF CAMBRIDGE
AUTHOR OF
A SHROPSHIRE LAD
BORN 26 MARCH 1859
DIED 30 APRIL 1936
GOODNIGHT. ENSURED RELEASE
IMPERISHABLE PEACE.
HAVE THESE FOR YOURS

AE Housman's ashes are buried here. To many people Housman will always be linked with Shropshire because of his volume of poems entitled A Shropshire Lad *but, in fact, he had no real connection with the county. He was born and educated in Bromsgrove in Worcestershire. From there he went to Oxford where he read Classics and later he became Professor of Latin at University College, London and then at Trinity College in Cambridge.*

A Shropshire Lad was published in 1896 and soon became popular because of its depiction and obvious love of the English countryside. It's said that more soldiers carried a copy of this book in their pockets than any other during the First World War – a constant reminder to them of the country they loved and were fighting to preserve.

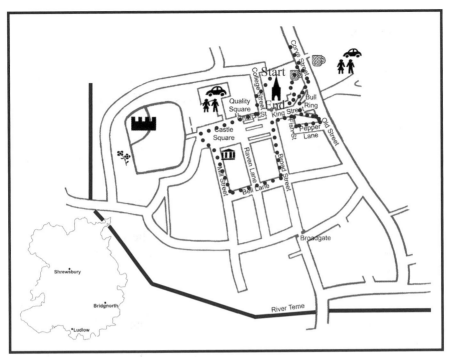

in England, reflecting the wealth of the merchants whose homes were in Ludlow. Indeed the north transept, just ahead of you, was built in the years just after the Black Death when generally the country was suffering from a severe economic downturn. This, in itself, is a reminder of the town's wealth.

Walk a little closer to the church, towards the north transept – can you see what appears to be an arrow embedded in the apex of the roof? It's a reminder that the Fletchers (or arrowmakers) Guild once had a chapel here.

Leave the churchyard through the small gate into College Street. Turn left and walk as far as the west door of the church. Stand so that you face the building across the street – Hosier's Almshouses. There have been almshouses (or "homes for the deserving poor") on this site since the late 1400s although this building dates from 1758. It was built by Thomas Farnolls Pritchard, best known in Shropshire as the man who probably designed the Iron Bridge.

John Hosier, after whom the building is named, was a cloth merchant in the town who gave money for the original almshouses here.

The tour continues along College Street into Church Street. If, however, it is late in the day and you wish to see the church before it closes, you would be advised to break off at this point and visit it first.

To continue the tour, turn right when you reach Church Street and walk to the end. Stop as you emerge into the open market area. In medieval times Ludlow's market was the same width as it is now but more than twice as long, extending behind you all the way to the Tolsey which you will see later. Looking ahead you can see the castle – it might now be ruined but still it dominates the market place and that was always intentional.

On the right is an entrance into an open courtyard. This is Quality Square. It's a lovely name and reminds us that once this was the plot for a very grand mansion where, in the 1590s, a lawyer named Charles Fox built his home. Unusually for the time it was built of brick.

From Quality Square continue walking towards the castle. Still regularly used for markets you may wish to use the time to browse for a while but eventually make your way to the castle entrance. Ludlow's castle is privately owned (it belongs to the Earls of Powis) but is open to the public and is a wonderful castle to explore.

The coat of arms shows the white lion of the Mortimer family, great Marcher lords from early medieval times. Castles they owned locally included those at Wigmore, Cleobury Mortimer and Chirk. Probably the best known member of the family was Roger Mortimer. Born in 1287, he acquired Ludlow Castle when he married Joanna de Geneville. He subsequently had an affair with Queen Isabella, wife of King Edward II, and it was probably Mortimer who was behind the murder of the King at Berkeley Castle in 1327. Mortimer then became Regent of England but, once the young King Edward III grew up and gained control, it wasn't long before Roger Mortimer found himself at Tyburn for his execution.

You would expect that this would have been the end of the family's power and ambitions but, several generations later, it was a descendent of Roger's who became King Edward IV. Edward IV's two sons were living in Ludlow when their uncle, Richard III, ordered that they be sent to the Tower of London from where they subsequently disappeared.

Notice also the feathers – these remind us of the link that the town had with Prince Arthur, Prince of Wales, the eldest son of King Henry VII. It was Arthur who was the first husband of Catherine of Aragon and the couple were living in Ludlow when he died.

There was no settlement of any size here in Saxon times. Following the Battle of Hastings, the Normans began to consolidate their power throughout the realm with the building of wooden motte and bailey castles, usually beside established towns. These castles were used both to guard the border as well as to control the newly-conquered populace. Before long many of these castles were replaced in stone.

Ludlow's castle was different. It was built rather later (in the 1080s) and was built of stone right from the start. If you go to explore it you will see the deep dry moat within that surrounds the main castle buildings; this was where the stone for the first castle was quarried.

As the centuries went by, Ludlow's castle grew in importance. Then, in 1485, Henry Tudor defeated Richard III at the Battle of Bosworth Field and became King Henry VII, thus uniting England and Wales. For the next couple of hundred years the town of Ludlow, and particularly its castle, became the centre from where the Marches and the principality of Wales were governed. The man in charge of law and order in the region was given the title of *Lord President of the Council in the Marches* and was answerable only to the monarch.

Eventually the castle fell into disuse so that in 1722, when he visited Ludlow, Daniel Defoe was to describe it as "the very perfection of decay". Some 50 years later it was decided that the castle should be totally demolished. Thomas Farnolls Pritchard was asked to prepare costings for the task. He wanted to save the ruin and so it is said that he deliberately undervalued all the stone and everything on the site while overestimating the cost of demolition. The job was therefore deemed to be too expensive and so, fortunately, the castle ruins were saved.

You may wish at this point to visit the castle. Alternatively, there is a very pleasant walk all around the outside walls that was first created as a promenade for local people in the early 1800s.

When you have finished your own exploration come back to this point and then turn so that you are facing the Square, looking over the market place. Towards the far end of the Square, there are the gable ends of three rather strange looking rows of buildings that look somewhat uneven and certainly unplanned. And that is exactly the case. They mark the places where early traders erected semi-permanent

61

stalls. As time went by those little stalls became permanent structures with narrow alleyways between; they're known as Butcher's Row, Shoemaker's Row and Lockier's Row - which tells you just what goods were once sold there.

Before moving away from the Square look out for the large stone building on the right with its timber-framed top floor – Castle Lodge. Although parts of it may be older, the stone building dates mainly from the late 16th century. Castle Lodge was the home of the governor of Ludlow Castle which may seem strange at first until you recall that the main castle building would have been occupied by the Lord President and his retinue. With many people from the borders, and from Wales too, coming to Ludlow to attend court cases, this building was used to house prisoners and it was once described as "such a place of punishment that the common people termed it a hell".

Continue the tour by walking from the Square and down Mill Street,

just beyond Castle Lodge. Stop when you are about a third of the way down the street. The large brick building that dominates the right-hand side of the street is the Guild Hall. It's not quite what it seems as, within it, there is a much older medieval structure dating back to 1411. It's said that when the original Guild Hall was built there was only one other building in the Marches that equalled it in grandeur – the Bishop's Palace in Hereford. It was remodelled in the 1700s when it was faced in brick.

Further down Mill Street, turn left when you reach Bell Lane, continuing until you reach the junction with Raven Lane. When the plots for properties were laid out the frontages faced Mill Street and Broad Street and these lanes would have given access to the back entrances. Our walk continues along Bell Lane into Broad Street but it's worth making a slight detour to walk up Raven Lane in order to look at the newly restored building on the left with its delightful modern carvings of local people.

Continue to Broad Street and stop so that you can look down the hill at the rear of the somewhat inaptly named Broad Gate, the only surviving medieval gateway into the town.

The tour continues up Broad Street. Give yourself time as you walk to look around you. On either side Broad Street is lined with grand mansions, predominantly dating from the 18th century although a number are older. Nikolaus Pevsner, author of the authoritative series of books on *The Buildings of England*, described this street as "one of the most memorable in England". This has always been (and still is) one of the smartest and most fashionable places to live in all of England.

Near the top of Broad Street, on the east side of the street, is the old Angel Hotel (now converted into apartments) where once Admiral Horatio Nelson stayed. The building at the top of the street is the Buttermarket. Built in 1743 at a cost of £1,000, it had a market on the ground floor whilst upstairs was the Town Hall. In 1785 the upper floor became home to the Blue Coat Charity School. The name derived from the fact that the poor children who attended were each given a coat to wear – apparently blue was the cheapest dye at the time.

The tour continues into the street to the right of the Buttermarket, King Street. As you make your way there take  time to admire the timber buildings on the corner with their intricate carvings. When it was built in 1403, Bodenhams would have sat right in the middle of the market place, implying that whoever built it was powerful enough to be able to ignore the town-planning restrictions that then applied. Sure enough, it was built by the Palmer's Guild, the most powerful guild in the town.

Walk along the right-hand side of King Street and take the first turning right into a narrow lane, Fish Street, which then bears left into Pepper Lane. Pepper Lane marks the southern edge of the open market that originally extended all the way from the castle to Old Street. Try to imagine just how large an area the market would once have covered.

On reaching Old Street stop once more. When the Normans arrived, not long after 1066, this area wasn't totally unoccupied. Old Street follows the line of an early road going down to a ford over the River Teme.

Walk up the hill and turn left just beyond the Olive Branch Coffee House. Stop to look at the building on the right. This is the Tolsey, so named because it was once the main toll house where traders coming into the town would have paid their tolls before being allowed to do business here. The building dates back to the 1400s but has been considerably altered over the centuries.

Walk around the Tolsey to look at the other side; the shop is called *Pie Powder*. This name comes about because the Tolsey was once used as a court of *pied poudre* meaning "dusty feet". In other words it served as a courthouse where people coming to the town on market days could bring their complaints (often boundary disputes with neighbours and the like) and have them heard before they even had time to brush the dust from their feet.

You are now standing in the Bull Ring, reminding us that this was where cattle were sold. Crossing King Street walk along the pedestrian street between two rows of houses just ahead. Some of the shops here still have their old Victorian frontages.

Emerging from this street you get an excellent view of the famous Feathers Hotel across the street. It was originally the home of a lawyer named Rees Jones, a man whose wealth is immediately apparent when you note the ornate carving all over the façade. His wealth wasn't just for outward show either – should you have the chance to go inside the hotel the plaster ceiling in the main sitting room upstairs is stunning. In 1670, however, the house became a coaching inn, with stabling behind it for 100 horses. Today, the Feathers is considered one of the finest old country inns in England.

Continue walking along Corve Street until you come to the point where the street suddenly widens. You've now reached the site of the north gate; the widening street reminds us that, outside the walls, there was more space for a wider road. From here retrace your steps, walking only as far as the Bull Inn. Turn into the courtyard.

Ludlow's oldest surviving inn, the Bull dates back to the 15th century. Notice the way the upper floor sticks out beyond the floor below. What you are looking at here could be described as an early motel – once, the rooms on the upper floor provided accommodation for guests while the ground floor provided stabling for their horses.

Ahead there is a short flight of stairs leading to a narrow passage. This is a right of way that takes you back to the churchyard near where you started the tour. Turn immediately left as you enter the churchyard and walk to the ornately carved timber building on the left.

This magnificent porch is the entrance to the Reader's House and dates to the early 1600s. The stone house attached to it, however, is much older and served for a time as the home of the school master appointed by the Palmer's Guild. By the time the porch was added it had become the home of the Chaplain for the Council in the Marches. Later it came to be used as the house for the reader, or curate, of the church, hence its present name.

To finish the tour, walk beyond the Reader's House as far as the porch of St Lawrence's Church. The porch is one of only two hexagonal church porches in the country (the other is to be found in Bristol). Whatever other buildings you find the time to explore while in Ludlow one building that you must not miss is St Lawrence's Church. It contains some magnificent stained glass but, to my mind, it's the misericords here that are special. A *misericord* is a carved shelf under a folding seat, designed for monks to lean on while standing for long periods during a service. Those in Ludlow are amongst the finest anywhere in the country. They date from the 1400s and are exquisite. Some show symbols of the church (as you would expect), others show scenes of daily life, some are delightful caricatures. Don't dare to leave Ludlow without seeing them!

Is this a window-tax window?
This tall, narrow window lighting all the floors is interesting as it's long been thought to be a window-tax window. When the tax on windows was in force the size of your windows wasn't considered; it was the number of windows in your house that you were taxed on. Recently it was discovered that this house wasn't built until 1838, just after the window tax was abolished. However, if I were building such a grand house I'm not sure that I would have trusted the government not to reintroduce the tax later and might well have had a window like this, just in case.

Market Drayton

The walk starts in the churchyard of St Mary's from where you can admire the view over the valley of the River Tern below. You will immediately understand why this town is situated here – it occupies an excellent hilltop defensive site.

The people who lived on the hill at the time of the Norman Conquest called their home *Draitune*, meaning a farm where loads were dragged. Who was dragging the loads, and what those loads consisted of, is a moot point these days. It may simply mean that, because the farm itself was on the top of a steep slope, then everything that was brought here then had to be dragged up the hill.

As happened throughout their newly conquered territories, the Normans immediately began to take control and in Draitune a castle was built just outside the town, guarding the road to Newport that you can see below. Nothing survives of that old castle except for the name of the farm – Tyrley Castle – that sits ahead of you, across the river. The castle didn't survive for long as, in the 12th century, the estate of Draitune was left to nearby Combermere Abbey.

Now turn around and study the church. The first church on this site was built in Saxon times. It was replaced by a stone building erected by the monks from Combermere Abbey. Those monks were very conscious of the rights they had been given over the running of this church so that, it is said, in 1280 when no less a personage than the Archbishop of Canterbury arrived, they refused to let him enter their church. It's difficult to know now exactly what happened but it would appear that the Abbot of Combermere had appointed a priest to serve the church, against the wishes of the Archbishop. Subsequently the local Sheriff arrived. He and his soldiers had orders from the Archbishop to forcibly remove the priest. A fight broke out, one man was killed and, as a result, the Abbot and six monks were excommunicated.

Today most people, when they eat gingerbread do so by slicing it and spreading it with butter. Apparently the correct way to eat it is to cut it into fingers and then dunk it in a glass of port. Incidentally, Henry VIII is reputed to have used ginger as an aphrodisiac!

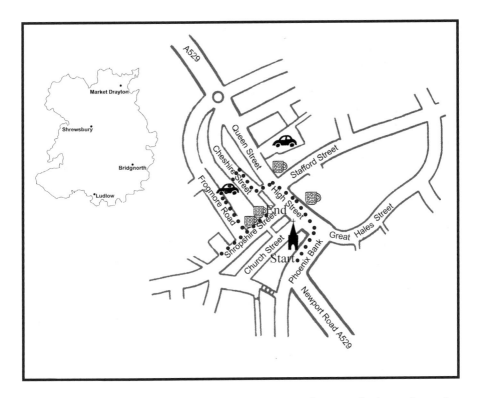

The church we see here today is rather later as it dates from the 1300s. By the 1700s it was described as being "greatly decayed" and it was estimated that £2,164 would be needed to repair it. Unable to afford such a large sum the townspeople patched up the church as best they could until, in 1884, the total church was restored at a cost of between £8,000 and £9,000. So that, if you have the time to go in and explore, you will find that it is Victorian in style.

Before moving on take time to look up at the tower. Local tradition has it that in the 1700s a seven-year-old boy once climbed up onto one of the gargoyles protruding from the top and then proceeded to pelt church-goers with excrement. That young boy was someone whom we will hear a lot more about on this tour – Robert Clive, the future conqueror of India.

From here walk to the south-east corner of the churchyard where there is a flight of steps. Stop at the top and look at the building ahead – the Old Free Grammar School. It's not known when the school was founded, but it was already in existence in 1555 when it was endowed with £22 by Sir Rowland Hill, then the Lord of the Manor. The boys who attended were

expected to learn English grammar and have an "understanding (of) the Latin, Greek and Hebrew languages". Incidentally, although called a "free" school, this did not mean that it cost nothing to attend; instead, in an age when most schools were firmly under church control, this one was free to run its own affairs as it wished.

One young boy who attended was Robert Clive. He was once described as "a fiery, unruly, yet lovable boy… At school he was the hero of everything but study". Always in trouble, Clive was eventually expelled (indeed, he was to be expelled from three schools altogether) but certainly at least one of his schoolmasters thought he showed promise saying of him that one day "few names would be greater than his".

Today the flight of stairs here is known as Clive Steps. Go down the steps and turn to your left to walk along Great Hales Street. Stop beside the building that sits on the left beside the next road junction. These days Market Drayton is synonymous with gingerbread. It's highly likely (though we don't know for sure) that it was Robert Clive through his associations with India who brought back recipes for highly spiced food, one of which was adapted to produce gingerbread. Whatever its origin, it was around 1817 when a Mr Thomas began to produce and sell gingerbread on this site using his own secret recipe. In 1864 the recipe and the business passed to a cousin, Richard Billington, and the family still produces gingerbread today – sadly not in Market Drayton but in Yorkshire.

Continue into the High Street and stop just beyond the Corbet Arms Hotel, by the next road junction. The hotel dates from the 18th century and one famous visitor who stayed here (in 1832) was Thomas Telford who was on an inspection tour when the Shropshire Union Canal was being built. Another person who once stayed here was Oswald Mosley who was born in Shropshire, at nearby Betton Hall, in 1896. While he was here the notorious fascist and 1930s political leader addressed crowds in the Square further up the street.

A more permanent occupant of the hotel is the ghost who haunts one of the rooms. She, so the story goes, was a chambermaid who was seduced by a young man who stayed here. He then scarpered which resulted in her committing suicide. It's said that she gets her revenge these days by disturbing the sleep of any bachelors who now occupy that same room.

Look along Shropshire Street, immediately to your left, and try to imagine it less than half its present width. It was once a little street known as the Shambles and lined with butchers' shops. The word *shambles* was originally always linked with streets where there were butchers because, in the days when animals were slaughtered and then carved up in the street, the mess would have always been considerable.

The street that you've just walked along once served as a natural conduit for rainwater falling further up the hill in the town. What with the mess from the butchering of animals and the effluent that was thrown into the street by those who lived along it, the whole area would have been somewhat putrid, to say the least. There is another story concerning that local hero, Robert Clive, that relates how, with a gang of fellow-hooligans, he terrorised the local people demanding protection money so that he wouldn't attack their properties. One butcher is said to have refused to pay. Clive and his gang therefore dammed up one of the natural streams that ran along here so that it flooded his shop.

It was here, too, that a local girl called Elizabeth Ann Lewis began her career lecturing on the evils of alcohol. She was an early follower of the Temperance Movement and was later to become known as the *Queen of Temperance*. Incidentally, her brother, John, refereed the very first English football Cup Final in 1872.

Cross the road and go and stand in the open paved area ahead, once a busy market place. The name Market Drayton, by which we know the town today, didn't appear in any document until the 16th century. However, the town had received its first charter to enable it to hold a weekly market as far back as 1245, in the reign of Henry III. That market still survives although these days, if you visit the town on a Wednesday, you will find that it takes over much of Cheshire Street where we will be going next. There were different kinds of markets in different parts of the town and here in the High Street was where, every September, the town's famous Damson Fair was held. Damsons would be piled into tin baths so that customers could check their quality. Such enormous quantities weren't for eating – the damsons were destined for Lancashire cotton mills where they were used as dyes. Modern chemical dyes saw the end of that trade but, if you walk along country lanes all around the town, you will still see numerous damson trees surviving along the hedgerows.

Before moving on, glance across the street and you will see the Crown pub on the corner of Stafford Street. King Charles I is said to have stayed here around 1645. Like so many other towns Drayton had a great fire. Its fire took place in 1651 and the Crown was one of the few survivors. Believe it or not, in the 1840s although the town had a population of less than 4,000 people, it was also home to 20 beer retailers, 13 taverns and public houses, and two wine and spirit merchants!

Now turn left to walk through the gap that leads into Cheshire Street. Immediately ahead of you, is the Buttercross market which dates from 1824. Notice the bell on the top. This was used to raise the alarm any time that there was a fire in the town. On hearing the bell, the local men would bring along a horse-drawn fire engine to put the fire out. The problem was that the horse was kept in a field at the bottom of Phoenix Bank (below the church) and the horse learnt to recognise the sound of the bell and would always run to the far end of the field as soon as it heard the ringing.

Streets were often named for the commodities that were sold in them – this street was once known as Horsemarket Street; others included Sheepmarket (now Stafford Street) and Stock Lane (now Queen Street). Despite its name the Buttermarket wasn't just used for butter; cheese was sold here too. In fact, cheese was one of the most important commodities sold in Market Drayton – this trade became particularly important in the 19th century with the growth of the industrial towns around Manchester and Liverpool and the need to supply them with food.

Walk along Cheshire Street until you are opposite the Library. The building that is now on your right dates from 1850 and was used as the town's Court House – most convenient for the solicitors offices in the same building.

The raven, from the coat of arms of the Corbet family, adorns the market. The Corbets came over with William the Conqueror and acquired large swathes of Shropshire. Their surname comes from the French word corbeau *meaning a raven, hence the raven that you see here.*

From here take the pedestrian way under the Library building and walk across the car park on the other side towards the Festival Drayton Centre (a former Methodist chapel that is now a community hall) on Frogmore Road.

On reaching Frogmore Road bear left and, when you come to Shropshire Street, turn right. Situated a little way from the hustle and bustle of the market area of the town, many people in the 1700s chose to build homes along this street and some rather fine examples still survive, although many have been altered over the years. Our walk takes us as far as the red pillar box from where you will need to retrace your steps.

The first house of interest is almost immediately on your right – Poynton House, dating from 1753. It was for a long time home to one of the oldest book clubs in the country, the club being founded in 1814. Further along, behind the pillar box, is Warren Court. Also an 18th century building it has now been converted into apartments. Turn around and look at the building directly opposite, on the south side of the street – Cotton's House. It dates from around 1600 and, at one time, was the home of a retired slave trader.

Walking back into town, the next house to look out for is No 41, The Old House, said to be one of the first brick buildings to be built in Market Drayton. Then, just past the junction with Frogmore Road, is The Red House at No 29. This was once the home of Captain William Wilkinson who served on the frigate *Sirius* at the Battle of Trafalgar. Because the *Sirius* had a shallower draft than the others in the fleet it was this ship that was used to sail close to the land of Cadiz Harbour and thus was the first to report to Admiral Lord Nelson when the combined French and Spanish fleet was leaving the port.

Just beyond the Red House is a timbered building known as the Abbot's House because it is said to have been here that the Abbot of Combermere Abbey would have stayed when visiting the town – this is unlikely since the building dates from after the abbey was dissolved, but perhaps there was an earlier building on the site that was used for that purpose. This building did, however, survive the 1651 fire only to be caught by another fire in 1991. Fortunately, the fire was only superficial and the main structure of the building survived allowing it to be subsequently restored.

Walk along to the end of the street where the tour ends beside the block of timber-framed buildings on the left - the Clive and Coffyne pub and the Tudor House Hotel. These buildings date from the period of rebuilding following the 1651 fire. The hotel has had a somewhat chequered history serving at different times as a variety of shops and even a bank. Finally, the

name of the pub is particularly interesting – Clive obviously refers to Robert Clive but what's a *coffyne*? This type of coffyne has nothing to do with wooden boxes but, instead, is a highly spiced meat pie, the recipe for which (like the gingerbread) was reputedly brought back from India by that great son of this town, Robert Clive himself.

Arthur Phillips

It was in Shropshire Street that Arthur Phillips set up a business as a bicycle manufacturer in the late 1800s. A brilliant mechanic he soon moved from bicycles to motor cycles and then to cars – he was the first man in Shropshire to repair a car. Once he drove from Shrewsbury to Market Drayton in a car preceded all the way by a man with a red flag. In later years Phillips became involved in the design of flying machines and some of his ideas were used by the Wright brothers when they designed their aeroplane.

Much Wenlock

The walk around Much Wenlock starts in the churchyard of Holy Trinity Church. There's a path along the south side of the church. Walk down this and stop at the end.

Near the end of the path there are two well-kept graves and if you look on the smaller you will see the name of William Penny Brookes. On the path itself there's a plaque with the words "Olympian Trail" on it and, as the tour progresses, you will see a number of these plaques all around the town so it would be as well to start by explaining what these are all about.

William Penny Brookes was born in 1809. He was a doctor and lived in Wilmore Street, just opposite the church. Dr Brookes was ahead of his time in that he was keen that his patients should exercise for the good of their general health. With this in view he inaugurated, in 1850, a local Olympic Games. Held annually in the fields beside the secondary school, it wasn't long before people from all over the Midlands began to join in, with thousands more attending to watch.

Brookes's Games weren't quite like the event we know today. Many of the races were more akin to primary school sports days – three-legged races, wheelbarrow races and the like. But it was a start and word of the Games soon spread abroad, reaching the ears of a Frenchman, Baron de Coubertin, who was later to copy the idea and make it international. Sadly, Coubertin's international Olympic Games were first held in 1896 and, as you will see from the date on the grave beside you, Brookes died just before.

The plaques are linked with a trail leaflet which is obtainable from the Visitor Information Centre and gives additional information about the town's association with the Olympic Games.

From here continue along the smaller path around the church leading to a metal gate. As you go you'll see, through the trees to the right, the ruins

William Penny Brookes did a phenomenal amount of good for the town of Much Wenlock – amongst other things he was instrumental in installing gas lighting, bringing the railway to Wenlock, building a market hall, a library and public reading room. He also served as a JP for many years. But today all these things are largely forgotten and it's his association with the Olympic movement that is remembered.

of Wenlock Priory. It was founded in the 7th century by a Saxon prince named Merewald. In an age when the sons of the nobility went fighting it was often the case that daughters were left in charge not only of their households but also of church institutions and this was the case here. Thus Merewald's daughter, Milberga, became the second abbess of what was then a dual house – in other words a monastery housing both men and women. Dual houses were quite common in Saxon times – it would have had entirely separate sections, even separate churches, for the men and the women with the whole enterprise run by a single person.

Like so many other Saxon monasteries this one suffered from Viking raids so that, by the 11th century, it was somewhat run down. Its fortunes were revived under the Normans when it was rebuilt as a single, male, institution. Subsequently dissolved in the reign of Henry VIII its ruins are now amongst the finest monastic ruins in Shropshire and worth exploring.

Meantime beyond the confines of the monastery the town of Wenlock began to grow. With the building of the new Norman monastery, a separate church was needed to serve the local people, Holy Trinity Church beside us. It's thought that it sits on the site of the Saxon church built to serve the female section of the first monastery.

Walk through the yard of the Priory Hall into the Bull Ring. You have to try and imagine this as an open area, stretching from the church behind and beyond the houses ahead. This was the original market area, outside the Priory gates. Over time people began to build around the edges and slowly these buildings crept up taking more and more of the space – the row of pretty cottages on the left date from the early 1600s while those houses on the other side are from the 1700s and 1800s – one building across the road, a former Savings Bank, has the date 1829 above the door.

If you wish to leave the tour and explore Wenlock Priory take the road to the right and you will find the entrance beyond the car park. Although now ruined the carving detail that survives gives a fine impression of just how beautiful a monastery it must once have been.

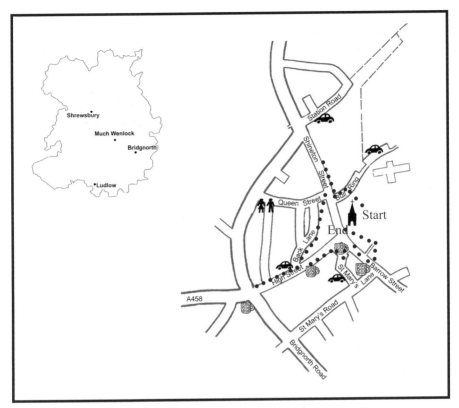

Otherwise, walk up the Bull Ring and turn right into Sheinton Street, going as far as the wonderfully named Bastard Hall on your right – apparently it is named after a family that once lived here, which does make one wonder! The very first programme for the popular television series, *Time Team*, was filmed here with the team researching just how old this building was. The timbers have been dated back to 1260 and, when first built, this house would have been one of the finest in Wenlock and used to house important visitors coming to the Priory who didn't wish, for whatever reason, to stay at the Priory itself. In those days, too, the house sat on the edge of the open market area that we've just been looking at.

It's a pretty name for a street but don't go by that. Once there was an open sewer running down the middle so that the name probably originated as Shit Street. In fact in 1797 Wenlock was described as "an ill-built dirty little place" and, a few years later, as "Muck" Wenlock.

From here retrace your steps (notice the Old Police Station on your left – now a private house) and turn right into Queen Street. Stop once again when you reach Back Lane, on the left, beside the timber-framed cottage on the corner. The well, now dry, that sits beside the house is dedicated to St Owen, a Frenchman who became Archbishop of Rouen. Local tradition has it that he visited St Milberga here in Wenlock – certainly he is known to have preached as far afield as Cornwall, Herefordshire and in the Channel Islands.

In fact one suggestion is that this is where the town gets its name – from Owen's *lock* or "dairy farm". I, however, much prefer an alternative explanation which says that the name comes from two Celtic words *gwen* and *loc* meaning "white church" which, perhaps, implies that the earliest Christian association with this site may even predate the Saxon monastery. Who knows?

While standing here do look at the gable end of the house beside you and notice the way in which the two main timbers seem to come from a single tree, sliced vertically and then leant together. A number of such pairings would have been used like this, linked together with horizontal beams to hold the structure together. This is a very early form of construction for timber houses and is known as a *cruck* house. Originally this house was a single storey building; there would have been a fire in the middle of the floor

and smoke would have made its way through the steeply slanting thatched roof on the top. At some time in its history an additional floor has been inserted and, to give more headroom upstairs, the outer walls have been extended.

Walk along Back Lane and turn right when you reach the High Street, beside the car park. The name Back Lane, by the way, tells us that this was once the outer perimeter of the old town. On reaching the High Street, stop beside Ashfield Hall, the first building on the right. It is said that Charles I stayed here in 1642 when making his way to the Battle of Edgehill. The house was then an inn, the Blew Bridge Inn. Previously, because of its situation beyond the town boundaries, there was a leper hospital here, or at least on the land beyond the large double gates.

The name Blew Bridge reminds us that this street once had a stream running down the length of it and, presumably, there was a bridge at this point.

Go as far as the end of the High Street and stop when you reach the busy main road. In medieval times the road from Bridgnorth would have turned off just up the hill to the left and entered Wenlock near the Raven Hotel which we will see later. The main road to Shrewsbury, on the other hand, left Wenlock along Sheinton Street, heading towards Wellington and crossed over the River Severn at Buildwas. This was to avoid the steep slope on Wenlock Edge which was then impassable to heavy wheeled vehicles pulled either by horses or bullocks. Around the turn of the 1700/1800s the road down the Edge was improved but it was still too steep for stagecoaches to use. This meant that people travelling to Shrewsbury by stagecoach still had to go via Wellington. But those who were in a hurry could leave the

stage in Wenlock and change to lighter horse-drawn carriages that could manage the steep road. The old coaching inn that you see across the road, took advantage of that traffic.

The pub was then known as the White Harte. It later changed its name to become the Wynnstay Arms and, as you can see, is now called the Gaskell Arms. You change your name as you change your allegiances.

Now retrace your steps to walk back down the High Street, cross the road when you get the chance and stop beside the Talbot pub. This street is lined with some wonderful examples of timber-framed buildings. Unfortunately, in many cases the oldest and most interesting parts are tucked away within the structure and inaccessible to the public. Across the road the beautifully restored Reynard's Mansion with its attractive balconies is a fine example. Look carefully above the windows on the right and you will see the date, 1682 – but this is a later addition built into what was once a much wider street and, in fact, the core of the building dates back to the early 1400s. That post and bar set between the two doors is a rest, used by porters to help them lift heavy loads onto their backs.

The Talbot pub, behind you, was known originally as the Abbot's House and was used also as a centre for almsgiving in medieval times. It's been here for at least 500 years.

Continue along High Street. The street was once known as Spittle Street – this isn't nearly as bad as it sounds, but is merely a contraction of "Hospital" Street. Stop once again when you are opposite the Corn Exchange which sits about half way along the street on the left. It's thought that there may once have been a hospital here which is the reason for the street's early name; another explanation could be that the street simply led to the leper hospital beyond the early town.

The Corn Exchange was built in 1852. Still regularly used as an open market area it also houses Wenlock's library. Notice the plaque dedicated to Dr Brookes on the wall.

Just before you reach the George and Dragon pub turn off the street into a narrow little passageway, the George Shut. This takes you to the rear of the pub where there would once have been the stables and the brewhouse where the ale sold in the pub was produced. Turn left almost immediately into Mutton Shut (named after a former pub called the Shoulder of Mutton). A *shut* is a Shropshire name for any small, narrow alleyway. There are numerous explanations for the name, the most likely being that since they were so narrow it was easy to erect a gate across the entrance to shut them when needed and so control access. Many of these shuts are now public rights of way.

Turn right when you enter Barrow Street and cross the road when you can, walking as far as the Raven Hotel. The Gaskell Arms that we saw earlier and the Raven have been rival inns for years. The Raven is the older, although even it is a replacement for an earlier Raven inn that once stood a little further away, next to a tollhouse where people coming to trade in

the town would stop to pay a toll and refresh themselves.

It was in the Raven that Baron Pierre de Coubertin was entertained in the 1890s when he came to Much Wenlock to see the Olympic Games. Today, if you take the opportunity to dine in the restaurant, you will see a number of early photographs on the walls that recall those early Games. Incidentally, the Much Wenlock

Olympic Games is still an annual event, held in July, and usually a representative of the Olympic Committee also attends in recognition that this was where the modern games began. On one occasion the Princess Royal attended the games in her capacity as a committee member.

Retrace your steps, turning right almost immediately into a little lane that looks like a private drive (but isn't). There's an old well against the wall on the right. This is St Milberga's Well dedicated to Abbess Milberga. There is a tradition that girls looking for a sweetheart would throw a crooked pin into the well and their wishes would be answered. St Milberga died in 722 AD and had obviously been highly successful as abbess because, by the time of her death, her monastery had become the wealthiest in the Saxon kingdom of Mercia.

Once you've made a wish of your own, go back to Barrow Street and turn right. Stop when you reach a little brick path that leads to the right, around the buildings that front onto the street, but take a moment first to look at the buildings on the other side of the road. Believe it or not, that little row of stone-fronted cottages is actually a row, or terrace if you like, of old timber, cruck houses. It's said to be the only cruck terrace in the world!

Now follow the path towards the churchyard. The houses that are now on your left are all without gardens which goes some way to explaining their history – they sit in the middle of what was once an open market area and probably began their life as semi-permanent stalls built within the market, which developed over the years to become large houses.

At the end of the path is the Guildhall. Walk through the covered passageway beneath it and then turn right. Go almost to the far end of the building until you reach the little window with a grill. Markets are busy places where trouble often breaks out if someone is accused of theft or cheating or even has too much to drink. Consequently, in medieval times lockups would be erected nearby and this happened here – the stone part of the Guildhall started life as a prison. In the 1570s the Guildhall was erected with one end sitting on the old prison.

It's said that the hall was erected in only two days. This sounds unlikely until you consider that buildings like this had all the timbers prefabricated elsewhere and these were then only brought onto the site once they were ready – so that, with a gang of men working together, the actual erection of the building could indeed have taken just two days. The ground floor was used as an open market and, with the prison so handy, it perhaps comes as no surprise to learn that the courthouse was upstairs – perhaps that also explains the presence of two sets of handcuffs attached to the front of the Guildhall.

Do go and visit the courthouse if you have the chance – there are displays in there about the history of the town and, my particular favourites, some wonderfully carved armchairs. The entrance is from the covered passageway that you have just walked through.

Finally, look across the road – today it's a pleasant open area in which to sit and people-watch but until around 150 years ago that little square was crammed with buildings. The clock in the centre commemorates Queen Victoria's Diamond Jubilee in 1897. Much Wenlock's museum is in the old Memorial Hall on the other side of the High Street and contains fascinating memorabilia concerning William Penny Brookes, amongst other things.

A talbot was an early breed of hunting dog from which present-day foxhounds have been bred. It was used as a badge of the Earls of Shrewsbury and there would once have been numerous pubs around the county with this name, a few of which survive today.

Newport

The tour of Newport concentrates on the area around the High Street. However, it is not just a walk up and down that street as there are one or two little loops along the way, one of which, by the canal, is particularly pretty and shouldn't be missed. Start the tour by making your way to St Nicholas's Church and stand with your back to the west entrance so that you are looking along the street.

Newport – the name implies a port (which seems a little odd in the heart of the country) that is new. Firstly, the word *port* in the early English language meant a trading place, not necessarily on the coast. So that when this settlement was first established in the 12th century it was done so in order to provide a local market and, at that time, it was certainly a *new* market.

Markets all around England usually had market crosses and Newport was no exception. Beside the cross people would meet, town criers would give announcements and, if you could get your pitch close by, it was almost guaranteed to be a good spot from which to sell your goods. Today all that remains of Newport's market cross is the base of the shaft.

But long before that market was established there were people living here. Indeed, the earliest evidence of settlement comes from the remarkable discovery locally of two prehistoric hollowed out log boats.

Around the same time that some Normans were setting up this little market town there was another group (monks in this case) setting up a religious establishment a couple of miles to the south – at Lilleshall Abbey. The land was marshy (it wasn't drained for agricultural purposes until the 18th and 19th centuries) and it wasn't long before the abbey came to be well known for its fishponds.

In an age of strict religious observance when no-one could eat meat on certain days or at certain times of the year, fish farms became an essential part of the food economy. Lilleshall Abbey flourished as a result and, inevitably, the people of Newport became involved in the same trade, hence the three fishes on the town's coat of arms.

By medieval times the town had the right (or perhaps, considering the expense, it was more of a burden) to supply the king with fish whenever he was in the area.

The Romans came this way too. Watling Street, linking London with Wroxeter, passes a short way to the south while a linking road to Chester passes to the east. These roads would have been used by Anglo-Saxon invaders seeking places to settle and establish farms and the first settlement of any size here was at Church Aston, just to the south of the town and now engulfed by present-day Newport.

Before moving on, turn around to look at the church. Newport's association with fish is evident here as the church is dedicated to the patron saint of fishermen, St Nicholas. Although the first church on this site was founded by the Normans, today's church was largely rebuilt in Victorian times, although the 14th century tower survives. If you do go inside look out for the fine window by William Morris and Edward Burne-Jones dating from the 1870s.

Still dominating the heart of the town, once St Nicholas's Church would have been islanded within the open market with buildings either side of a wide street. Today the market space has been encroached upon by the buildings next to the old market cross. Start the tour by walking through the alley between the church and those later buildings and you step back in time into St Mary's Street. Writing in the 1950s Nicholas Pevsner said of Newport that "from the point of view of townscape there is nothing better in North Shropshire than Newport". I cannot agree with him regarding much of the High Street, which we will see later, but St Mary's Street, with its quaint buildings and cobbled road surface, is delightful.

Turn left in St Mary's Street and walk as far as the Royal Victoria Hotel. With the introduction of regular and reliable stagecoach services in the 1700s, Newport became an important stop for coaches travelling between London and Chester. Small coaching inns may have served most travellers but anyone of note would have wanted to stay somewhere in style and it was for this trade that the hotel was first built.

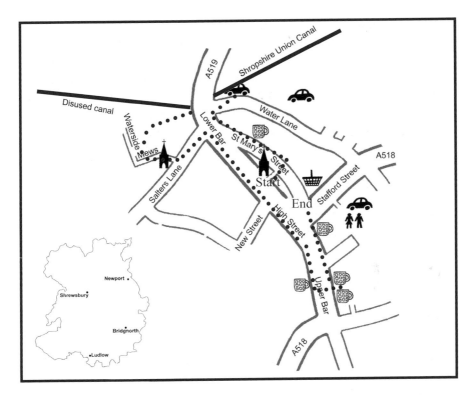

Originally opened in 1830, two years later a young Princess Victoria passed through the town with her mother, the Duchess of Kent. They only stopped for lunch but, before continuing on their way, the Princess agreed that the new hotel could take her name.

Continue walking along the street as it joins the High Street and look out as you go for a milestone built into the side of a building, now a funeral directors. It tells us that London is 141 miles away from Newport. Look at it carefully and you may be able to detect rust – the milestone is made of iron.

At around this point, the High Street changes its name to Lower Bar, an indication that it was here (beside Mischa's Restaurant) where, in medieval times, you would have reached the northern boundary of the town. Walk just beyond the restaurant and turn back to look at the side of the building (above the conservatory) and you will see that the house has an interesting history. At one time it was a two-storey building with a steeply pitched roof, clearly defined in the brickwork. Then, in the 18th century an additional floor was added and the roof flattened. This happened to houses all over the country at this time but it's not always as easy to detect as it is here.

When you reach the road junction with Water Lane turn right and walk into the car park on the other side of the road towards the old canal. For a short time in its history Newport really could be described as a port with goods coming in and out on water – in this case on the Newport-Shrewsbury Canal, as it was then called. The canal was opened in 1835 but, sadly, lasted for only a century, closing in 1926.

A small section of the canal has recently been restored. To explore it walk under the road bridge. Mind your head – where once there was a canal with space for narrow boats this has now been filled in and there is hardly any headroom at all. Beyond the bridge turn around and have another look – you've just walked under what is known as a *roving bridge*. When the canal was first built the narrow boats were all pulled by horses. At junctions with other canals or roads or where the horses needed to change from one side of the canal to another, it was often difficult for the horse to continue to pull the narrow boat without getting the rope tangled – however this bridge has been ingeniously designed so that a horse pulling a narrow boat could cross over from one side of the canal to the other without the tow rope having to be untied.

There is a very pleasant walk along by the old canal here and you may wish to explore further. But, to continue the tour, follow the gravel path and, just where the hedge on your left ends, you will see that the path forks. Take the left path up a slight slope leading into a housing estate. Walk through the estate (it's called Waterside Mews) to Salters Lane. Just before reaching Salters Lane there's a high brick wall on the right. It surrounds Salter's Hall, now the presbytery for the Roman Catholic Church of Saint Peter and Saint Paul. The original Salter, who gave the road its name, was probably Judge Salter who lived in a house on this site in the mid 1400s. Subsequently the property passed to the family of the Earls of Shrewsbury and it was they, a leading Roman Catholic family, who altered the house in 1789 and used it as the home for a Catholic chaplain serving the local community, the first licensed Catholic Chaplain in Shropshire since the time of the Reformation.

Turn left in Salters Lane and when you reach Lower Bar once again, turn right. As you will have already noticed, this part of the High Street is lined on both sides with some fine Georgian buildings. The first one you pass now is Roddam House and, like Mischa's Restaurant across the road, it too, is an older house (dating from the 1600s) with a Georgian façade. It's name comes from Mary Roddam, a local philanthropist who formed the Newport Nursing Association and was instrumental in turning this house into a maternity home in the early 1900s.

Next door is Beaumaris House. It was once an inn called The Bear and Charles Dickens is said to have stayed here. Perhaps it was during his visit that Dickens heard of a local recluse called Elizabeth Parker, the inspiration for Miss Havisham in his *Great Expectations*.

Just beyond Beaumaris House you come to the first of two pairs of almshouses, each with a plaque stating that they are for "two single" men or women and were founded by William Adams. I particularly enjoy the comment on how they were repaired "and beautified" in 1821.

William Adams was born in Newport but made his fortune in London as a haberdasher. A haberdasher was a merchant who primarily sold sewing implements (pins and needles etc) along with things like ribbons and buttons, sometimes even items such as gloves and hats. Adams didn't just found the almshouses, he also established the school that sits between them. This was in 1656 and Adams had to get permission from Oliver Cromwell in order to set it up. When Charles II subsequently claimed the throne, an Act of Parliament was passed to confirm the terms of the school's foundation.

William Adams also endowed his school with a 900-acre estate at Knighton in southern Shropshire and a library of 1,400 books, then one of the largest libraries in the country. Sadly, only seven of those 1,400 books are still owned by the school today. Imagine how useful that library would have been to a young Samuel Johnson – tradition has it that he applied for a post working for the headmaster of the time, the Reverend Samuel Lea, but was turned down. Dr Johnson once proudly commented on the fact that Lea was later to remark that "it was his greatest claim to fame that he almost taught Johnson".

Continue walking along the High Street and stop when you reach Partridge Opticians on the right, opposite the market cross. Like so many other towns around the country this one, too, suffered from fire – Newport Great Fire took place in 1665. In order to try and limit the risk of fire was already the law that houses within towns should have slate or tile roof – which makes this building curious because it has wooden shingles on part of the roof, on the turret at the corner. Not only that, but it has the date 166 on the side, just after the fire.

Next cross over New Street. Once known as Pig Fold because swine markets were held here, with the gentrification of the town in the 1800s it perhaps no wonder that that name was changed.

There are in Newport one or two buildings that survive from before the 1665 fire. One is No 75 which, despite its later frontage, dates from the 1500s – peek down the alleyway beside it and you can see the early timber framing.

Now walk down the street until, just past the Adams House Hotel you reach the Guildhall, one of the oldest buildings in Newport, dating from the late 1400s. On reaching the Guildhall you are almost at the edge of old Newport, Upper Bar. Upper (and Lower) Bar were probably so-called because people coming into the town would have had to pass a bar or gate where they would have been charged a toll for the privilege of trading here. Inevitably, many would have travelled a fair distance to reach Newport and on arrival, the first thing they wanted would have been somewhere to quench their thirst and, sure enough, there are a number of pubs here – such as the Pheasant and the Shakespeare just across the road. The earliest record of the Pheasant goes back to 1672.

Cross the road on the pedestrian crossing and then walk back along the other side of the High Street. You'll pass yet more (former) pubs as you go. Barber's Estate Agents was once the Star – they even still have the old star sign hanging above the entrance. Boots' Pharmacy also still has a hanging sign although this is now used for their pharmacist's cross;

was once the Raven and Bell. Across the road Temperton & Temperton was another pub, The Old Bell, as was Barclays Bank. Eventually you reach a pub that actually survives, the Barley Mow, or Barley as it is known these days.

Cross over Stafford Street just beyond the Barley and stand in front of the Market Hall, turning to look back along the High Street. When the Normans arrived and established their town and market they planned their "new port" with precision. This wide, open area was where once the cattle markets, sheep markets, horse markets and so on were held. Today the space is taken over by cars, vans and buses. Along either side of the market area the Normans carefully measured out building plots and, if you study the widths of the frontages of the present shops, you can still appreciate the regularity of that early town planning.

Those early markets may have gone but there's still a market here – in the building on your left. The market hall was built in 1860 on the site (perhaps not so surprisingly) of two former pubs. The market still flourishes - so why not finish your tour of Newport by exploring it.

Famous old boys of Adams Grammar School
There have been many boys taught here who went on to achieve great things. Amongst them are some rather interesting politicians. One was Robert Charnock who grew up to become an ardent supporter of the Roman Catholic King James II and as a result attempted to kill King William III. He failed in this and was hanged for treason.

Another was Thomas Parker who became Lord Chancellor. When, in 1714, Queen Anne died and her successor had still not arrived from Germany, Parker briefly became Regent of Great Britain – he was therefore the last non-royal to act as Sovereign in British political history. Parker was raised to the peerage, becoming Earl of Macclesfield in 1718. He became fabulously wealthy but, in 1725, he was impeached for corruption, having taken more than £100,000 in bribes – that would be the equivalent of something like £11 million these days, which rather puts modern parliamentary scandals in their place! He was fined £30,000 and placed in the Tower of London until he paid but, since all his money had been illegally acquired and therefore confiscated, he no longer had the wherewithal with which to pay! He was released after six weeks and spent the rest of his life in relative obscurity.

I hasten to add that not all the famous old boys of Adams are rogues! There have been a number of bishops amongst them, as well as leading scientists, academics and even a Radio One disc jockey.

Oswestry

The tour of Oswestry starts beside St Oswald's Church. Because of its dedication to a saint killed nearby in the 7th century, there's probably been a church here from early times. In early medieval times the town was referred to as *Blanc Minster*, the "white church" so perhaps it was then whitewashed. To that white church a tower was added, sometime around 1200 which, four centuries later, was to serve as a lookout post during the time of the Civil War when the entire building was seriously damaged. It was subsequently rebuilt and then restored in Victorian times.

Before leaving the churchyard look for the Oswestry Visitor Centre in Holbache House. It was this building that housed the original Oswestry College, one of the oldest schools in England, founded by David Holbache (a lawyer) in 1407. Used today as a coffee shop as well as a visitor centre, it is still possible to see the old schoolrooms upstairs. As you would expect, subjects then included Latin, Greek and English Grammar. However, one subject on the curriculum was archery and it's interesting to note that money was put aside for pupil entertaining, the entertainment being cockfighting. The school came to the attention of both Queen Elizabeth I (who gave it an annual endowment of forty shillings) and Oliver Cromwell. Cromwell had the headmaster at the time (this was in 1657) dismissed for being "too delinquent" – a delightful description for a headmaster until you realise that, in fact, he was "too Royalist" for Cromwell's tastes!

Leave the churchyard, walking into Church Street and turn left. Pause when you are standing opposite the Wynnstay Hotel. It was once called The Cross Foxes (from the badge of the Wynnstays, a powerful local family) and,

---

Oswestry

It's not very often you find a town with a name that can be dated to a specific event. Oswestry is just such a town. The year was AD 642. This area was then part of the Saxon kingdom of Mercia, ruled by the pagan King Penda. Somewhere near here he fought a battle, the Battle of Maserfield, against the Christian king of Northumbria, King Oswald. Oswald was killed and, following the battle, his body was hacked to pieces and the pieces hung up in a tree on the battlefield. That is where the town's name came from – Oswald's tree.

But the story continues. An eagle came down and picked up one of those bits of King Oswald and flew off with it. A few hundred yards away the eagle dropped his find; Oswald's limb fell to the ground and, where it hit the ground, a miraculous well sprang up. As a Christian killed in battle fighting a pagan, Oswald was promptly venerated as a saint. This miraculous well thus became a holy shrine for Christians.

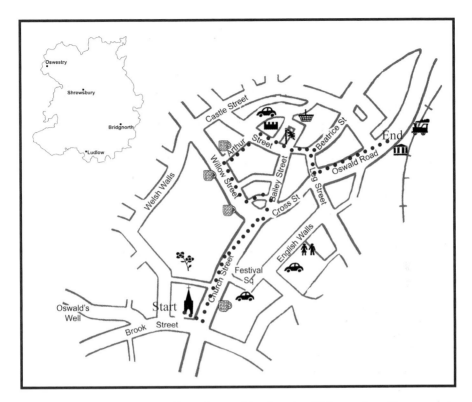

at another time, The Bowling Green (the hotel still has a bowling green). Built in the 1700s to serve as a coaching inn, it later was to become one of the main hotels along the London to Holyhead Road. On one occasion Princess (later Queen) Victoria stayed here. Apparently the crush of local people standing outside the building to try and see her was so great that one lady was killed.

Walking along Church Street you pass the town's war memorial, the splendid Cae Glas Park gates. The name comes from the house that once stood here; it was demolished in the 1830s and the materials used to build the houses that now stand on either side of the garden.

Just beyond the gates, on the right is Festival Square. The statue of a Border farmer is well worth a look. It is by Ivor Roberts Jones, who was born in Oswestry in 1913 and is probably best known for his statue of Winston Churchill in Parliament Square in London. This reminder of livestock markets is particularly appropriate here because the square was once the site of the town's cattle market.

As you continue along Church Street look carefully for two unusual features on the right hand side of the road. Firstly, tucked between two shops (a delicatessen and a butcher) is a carved stone column with the words "Toll Thorough" and the arms of the Earls of Powis inscribed on it. This marks the spot where once you would have passed through a toll gate when you came into the town.

Just beyond it, look up and you will see a carved three-legged white horse set into the brickwork. At one time this building was a pub called The White Horse and the story of how the horse came to have only three legs is rather amusing. There was a riot in Oswestry in 1832 following a local election and one of the rioters climbed up, pulled the leg off the carving and hurled it through the window of one of the more unpopular candidates.

The road junction at the end of Church Street is known as The Cross because there was once a market cross here, long since removed to allow an easier flow of traffic. The white building diagonally across the road first served as an indoor market and then, believe it or not, was used during the Second World War as a store for ammunition. Today only the façade of this market survives. The inscription above the door is in Latin and translates as: *Time and money, space and weight,*
By one fixed standard calculate.

Cross the road bearing right into Cross Street and go and stand opposite the large timber-framed building, Llwyd House, sitting beside the junction of Cross Street and Bailey Street. Standing as it does so close to the English-Welsh border, Oswestry was regularly attacked by one side or another through history. This constant fighting, however, meant that the town suffered many fires so that, sadly, there are few truly old buildings in the town, one of the oldest being Holbache House. In fact, one part of the town just beyond the Wynnstay Hotel was for a long time known as *Pentrepoeth* or "the burnt end" following a fire in 1567, although that particular fire may have been accidental.

Nevertheless, there are one or two interesting survivals and this is one. Llwyd Mansion was built in 1604 as the town house of John Lloyd a local landowner and merchant. Particularly interesting is the carving that adorns the house – it's a two-headed eagle, the badge of the Emperor of Austria. An earlier member of the family was given permission by the Emperor to use the badge after he had distinguished himself fighting during the Crusades.

Look up Bailey Street – as its name implies, it once led to the bailey of Oswestry's castle. Our route, however, leaves this street almost immediately, turning left along a narrow alleyway, Clawdd Du, just behind the Abbey bank. This takes you behind the former market hall (or ammunition store) seen earlier.

Emerging into Willow Street almost opposite you will see a pub named for Wilfred Owen – he was born in Oswestry in 1893 and grew up to become one of the finest of the First World War poets. Sadly he was killed on 4 November 1918, just a week before the Armistice.

Turn right and walk up Willow Street, stopping when you reach the Five Bells pub. This was the birthplace of another soldier, Harold Whitfield. He was awarded the Victoria Cross in 1918 after he single-handedly charged and captured a Lewis gun, killing the entire gun crew, and then turned their gun on the enemy. He died in 1956.

If you care to walk further along the street, as far as No 55, you will find the birthplace (in 1869) of Sir Henry Walford Davies. He became a chorister at St George's Chapel, Windsor Castle, and later organist of the private chapel in Windsor Great Park. In 1934 he was appointed Master of the King's Music.

Our walk, though, leaves Willow Street through a little lane, Arthur Street, just before the Last Orders pub. This pub is thought to be one of the oldest in Oswestry yet it also once served as a place of worship. In 1672 a Royal Licence was obtained allowing the use of one of the rooms in the pub for worship by members of a nonconformist chapel, the first of its kind in the town. Nearly one hundred years later a new chapel, Christ Church was built, further up the hill on the left, on the site of the former town gaol. Renamed the Kingswell Centre, it's now a community and arts centre.

Beyond Arthur Street is the entrance to Oswestry Castle which would once have dominated the entire town. In fact you are already within the bounds of the medieval castle – the hillock opposite is merely the site of the

former motte that stood within a much larger castle. The first wooden castle here was one of many protecting newly conquered Norman England from both Welsh incursions and also from possible rebellions from the recently cowed English. In deed, Oswestry changed hands many times in its history so that it was probably the Welsh who began building the first stone castle on this site in 1148.

With the linking of England and Wales under the Tudors you might expect that the military importance of the castle would decline. However, Oswestry was to see warfare once again during the Civil War when the town was besieged by Parliamentarians when, as mentioned earlier, the church suffered considerable damage. Finally capturing the castle, the Parliamentarians destroyed its main gate using an early form of landmine to blow it up and then *slighted* it. Slighting is the term given when castles were deliberately destroyed in order to ensure that they couldn't be put to military use again.

If you have the time, do go and climb to the top where there are excellent views of the town and you will see what little remains of a once large castle. The area was turned into public gardens in 1890 to commemorate Queen Victoria's jubilee three years before.

It's a pretty name but how it was derived is not known. Some have suggested that it comes from the "road to Wales", others that the name derives from the town's "walls" but, since it goes through the walls rather than following the line of them I expect that, if either explanation is correct, it is more likely to be the first one.

Before leaving the castle, look closely at the pillars positioned either side of the steps and you may be able to make out the words "Toll Through" carved on them – there was never a toll payable to enter the castle and, instead, these stones once stood by the toll gate in Beatrice Street.

From here walk beyond the castle to Bailey Head. This large, open area once served as an outer bailey for the castle. The keep on the mound would have been the stronghold of the castle but castles needed areas for stables, armouries, kitchens, stores, barracks for the men etc. Also important was the need for a market place close to the castle where traders could be forced to pay dues for trading and so, over the centuries, this area developed to become Oswestry's market.

To the left the building at the top of the street, typical of many unfortunate 1960s designs found all over the country, is today's market hall. The present building replaced a Victorian Corn Exchange and Wholesale Cheese and Butter market.

Once, those who were caught cheating or thieving in the market would have been punished in the open market – where the stocks and whipping post would have been. Today, instead, infringements of the law are dealt with in the Magistrate's Court in the Guildhall. The Guildhall is the large building between Arthur Street and the market hall. It was built in 1893 at a cost of £11,000. Notice the carved relief on the left depicting King (or Saint, if you prefer) Oswald.

Walk down the hill along Bailey Street and take the first turning left, Albion Hill. Stop when you reach the junction with Leg Street and look along the street ahead, Beatrice Street. The northern gate of the town once stood, just around the corner. If you care to walk a little way along the street look out for the Fighting Cocks (a former pub) which is thought to be one of the oldest buildings in the town, dating back to the 1300s.

Turn to the right to walk down Leg Street towards the traffic signals.

In November 1970 a new shop opened on part of the site now occupied by Martin Britten's Clubhouse. The two men who opened this shop selling frozen foods were already employees of the local branch of Woolworths and when it was discovered that they were moonlighting they were promptly sacked. This, however, meant they could concentrate on their new business. That shop was the first branch of Icelands – it had been established with an initial capital outlay of just £60 (enough to cover the first month's rental on the shop premises) and now has outlets all over the country.

Built in the 1800s, this building was once the Queens Hotel accommodating the growing number of travellers passing through the town once the London-Holyhead Road was opened. Fortunately, when the stagecoach service declined with the later opening of the railways, the hotel found it had been built in just the right place to benefit from that trade too.

Finish the walk by crossing over the road here and going down Oswald Road towards the former station. The railways have played an important part in Oswestry's history – the town was once the headquarters of the Cambrian Railway with a thriving engineering and maintenance centre. The company was to become a major employer in Oswestry yet when the idea of a railway to the town was first suggested no-one had wanted one. Consequently land was obtained for the new line to be built to the east with a station at Gobowen and it was only later that an extension was built to link Oswestry with the system – which is why, following the railway cuts in the 1960s, the town is once again served by the station at Gobowen, three miles away.

Today the station survives as a tea-room where our tour ends, and Oswestry's railway heritage is remembered in the museum beside it.

It is thought that the name Beatrice came from two words – badde meaning "poor" and ric meaning "a stream" or "a ditch". In other words it refers to the sewer that would once have run near the street here and into which local people would have thrown their effluent and goodness knows what else besides. It was often the case that sewage was deliberately allowed to build up in such ditches until a crust formed over it all, by which time it was considered to have become fully matured and ready for use as manure.

Shrewsbury

The tour of Shrewsbury starts by Shrewsbury Castle. If you wish go up to the top of the hill to Laura's Tower, the path is just within the main entrance, on the right. Walking to the top and looking at the views all around goes a long way to explain why Shrewsbury is here.

We have no idea how old the town of Shrewsbury is; all we know with any certainty is that there was a town here, and an important one too, by the time of the Norman invasion in 1066. Whoever it was who founded the settlement (perhaps his name was Scrobbe) recognised that this was an excellent defensive site on a hill with a river almost completely encircling it. And so, Scrobbe's *byrig* (or fortified place) was founded. However, another interpretation of the town's name is that it was "the fortified place with lots of shrubs".

By the time the Normans reached *Scrobbesbyrig*, there was already a thriving market town here and they promptly built a castle from which they could control the local people and protect the border against Welsh incursions. That first castle was a wooden one, probably covering much the same area as the castle and its grounds do today. By the turn of the century, it was rebuilt in stone.

Shrewsbury Castle was one of many guarding the English-Welsh border. Over the years it grew until, at one point, its bailey covered an area reaching half-way up Castle Street. It was a virtual ruin by the time England and Wales were united under the Tudors and it then became a private home.

Romantic it may be, but Laura's Tower isn't that old. It dates from the late 1700s when it was built by Thomas Telford as a coming of age gift for Laura, the daughter of the then MP for the town, Sir William Pulteney.

It was at this time that the row of windows along the top of the building were inserted. Briefly refortified during the Civil War, it began to crumble once again until, towards the end of the 18th century, Sir William Pulteney employed the engineer, Thomas Telford, to restore it as a suitable home. Sir William Pulteney was the MP representing Shrewsbury at that time and needed a home in the town.

Subsequently, the castle was acquired by Shrewsbury Corporation in 1924 and today it serves as a military museum for Shropshire regiments.

Leave the castle and walk to the (private) parking area and stop where you can study the large building across the road, Shrewsbury's Library. When Henry VIII dissolved all those monasteries in the early 1500s he, at the same time, obliterated an entire education system so that many new schools were subsequently founded. Shrewsbury School was founded in 1552 and originally was situated in a timber-framed building, parts of which still survive within the present library.

The school has had a chequered history. By the 1590s it was the largest in England but come the 1700s its reputation had fallen drastically, and it wasn't until the early 1800s that a new headmaster, Samuel Butler, restored its reputation.

The list of famous old boys is varied and includes "Bloody" Judge Jeffreys and (in more recent times) Michael Heseltine and Michael Palin, along with the fictional Sir Sidney Carton, hero of Charles Dickens's novel, *A Tale of Two Cities*. But undoubtedly, the best-known of all the former schoolboys is Charles Darwin (born in Shrewsbury in 1809) whose statue sits in front of the entrance. He attended the school during Butler's time but didn't impress his headmaster at all – here was a boy whose interests were almost entirely concentrated in natural history at a time when the school curriculum would have been totally classics based. The two would never have agreed.

Walk past the 19th century Presbyterian church (now home to *Women in Mind*) and stop immediately so that you can look up to the left at the lovely timber gatehouse with its elaborate carving detail. In Tudor times, once England and Wales were finally united, the post of Lord President of the Council in the Marches was introduced. The Lord President, based in Ludlow, controlled law and order in the entire Marches (or borders) region.

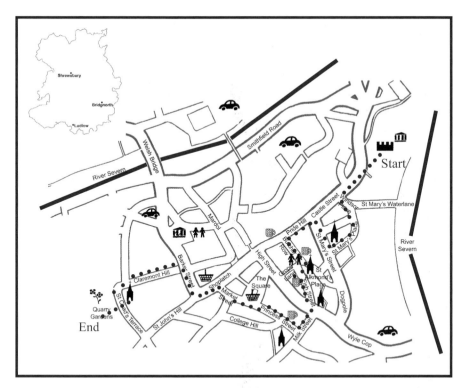

However, such an official needed to travel throughout his administrative region and, when in Shrewsbury, would stay in the building that you see through the gateway, known as the Council House. The best known Lord President was Sir Henry Sidney whose son, Philip, attended Shrewsbury School. Philip Sidney died as a result of wounds received fighting for the Dutch against their Spanish oppressors at the Battle of Zutphen in 1586. This Shrewsbury link with Zutphen is reinforced today, as the two towns are now twinned.

Continue walking along Castle Street and take the first turning on the left into Windsor Place. There's a fork in the road just ahead – go and stand on the pavement between the two roads and turn to look back the way you

The inscription over the entrance to Shrewsbury Library is Greek and translates as "He who loves learning will become learned" – most apt for both a school and a library.

have come. Notice the road sign, St Mary's Water Lane, and the name of the restaurant, *Traitor's Gate*. The two names are both used by locals for the narrow lane that leads down to the river, reminding us of the time in the Civil War when Shrewsbury was attacked by Parliamentary soldiers. Local tradition has it that some of the soldiers entered the town through the gate at the bottom, which a traitor deliberately left open. Unfortunately, there is no documentary evidence to support this story but there is often more than a grain a truth in such tales so who knows what really happened here…

Continue along Windsor Place turning right into St Mary's Place and walk to the west door of the church. If you possibly can, you must take time to explore this church. Sadly, it's now redundant and therefore is open only when there are volunteers to man it, all of whom will be delighted to tell you about its history. It is, incidentally, still a consecrated church and occasional services are held here.

St Mary's was a Saxon foundation and is typical of churches up and down the country which have developed through the centuries and show signs of many periods and styles of architecture. Look up at the steeple. Notice how the top appears to be cleaner stone than the rest. This is because the original steeple collapsed in a storm in 1894. The accident to the steeple co-incided with the time when Shrewsbury's townsfolk were raising money to erect the statue of Charles Darwin outside the Library. Apparently, the vicar here disagreed with Darwin's theories to such an extent that, following the disaster to his church, he then preached a sermon in which he said that the disaster was a judgement on the local people for daring to raise the funds for such a memorial.

Leave the churchyard by the main gate, turn right and walk to Pride Hill, crossing the road at the pedestrian crossing. Stand by the cross and look down along the street. It was somewhere here, beside an earlier market cross, that David, Prince of Wales, was executed in 1283. Captured in Wales fighting against his overlord, King Edward I, David was brought to Shrewsbury and tried for treason. Inevitably found guilty, he was subsequently executed at the top of Pride Hill.

Walk on down Pride Hill, stopping half way down the street beside the junction, on the left, for Butcher Row. Before turning into Butcher

Row, pause first to look at the row of buildings on the right-hand side of the street. Being a border town, Shrewsbury was constantly under attack from the Welsh. Things got so bad that eventually the early fortifications were replaced by stones walls which are now enmeshed in the foundations of all the buildings you see. It may amuse you to learn that one of the best places to see what survives of those medieval walls is in the basement of McDonalds. Go and have a look.

Turn into Butcher Row and go as far as the entrance to the Prince Rupert Hotel. Given the name of the street it won't surprise you to learn that this was where once meat markets were to be found. Can you see the meat hooks still surviving above the word *Mystique* on the Abbot's House, across the road?

The Abbot's House was erected in "c1450". In fact the timbers within the building have been dated using a scientific technique known as *dendrochronology*, or tree-ring dating, and we know therefore that the trees were cut down in 1457/58. There is also documentary evidence that tells us that the building was completed in 1459. Confirming each other as they do, these dates are incredibly important as they also serve to confirm other dendrochronology dates obtained for buildings elsewhere in Shropshire.

The Abbot's House, incidentally, has nothing to do with Shrewsbury Abbey. Instead it was owned by the Abbey of Lilleshall, along with a number of other properties here and in nearby Fish Street. Lilleshall Abbey was particularly well known for the production of fish and would have sold it here, which explains why Fish Street is so named. Talking of names – the Prince Rupert Hotel is named for Prince Rupert, a nephew of Charles I, who had his headquarters here for a time during the Civil War years.

Bear left through what was once the old cattle market towards St Alkmund's Church. Stop beside the low hedge. St Alkmund, to whom the church is dedicated, is a truly obscure saint. The son of a Northumbrian king, he was martyred in Mercia in AD 800. His relics were brought to Shrewsbury from Derby by Ethelflaeda, daughter of King Alfred and it was she who founded the church around AD 912 – it was probably felt that the

relics would be safer here, further away from the risk of Viking attack.

Today's church is particularly interesting architecturally for its windows or, at least, for the three iron windows, one of which is directly ahead of you. They date from the late 1700s, a time when the Industrial Revolution was at its height and Shropshire led the world in innovation. Sadly, the Victorians thought them unsightly and changed the others to the plain stone-framed windows.

Now turn slightly to your right to look at the timber building. It was decided in the 1960s that it should be demolished and already a section on the right (where the present-day public toilets are) had been pulled down when it was realised that what was being destroyed wasn't a 17th century tumble-down cottage but, in fact, a fine example of a medieval hall house. In the end what survived of the building was restored, being almost entirely replaced in the section on the right, although to the left you can see a lovely mix of new timbers with old. Notice the date on the left – 1971 – the date the building was restored although parts of it are known to date back to at least the 1500s.

Walk down the steps in the middle of the building – known as Bear Steps they are named for a pub called the Bear that was once just opposite – and turn left in Fish Street. Stop near the Three Fishes pub (the sign reminds us that this was once the property of Lilleshall Abbey) and look up at the church ahead, St Julian's, with its different colours of stone.

You may have noticed the same effect at St Mary's Church. These towers look odd to us today but what we don't realise is that, when these early additions were originally made, they were never intended to look different. In all probability they would have been painted, plastered or, at the very least, whitewashed so that the change in the colour of the stone would have been immaterial.

Continue to the end of Fish Street, cross over the High Street at the bottom and walk along Milk Street. Turn right into Princess Street and stop when you reach the passage beside the Golden Cross Inn. That odd looking structure that you see on the hillock across the road is all that now remains of Old St Chad's Church. It's possible that the first settlement in Shrewsbury was hereabouts and indeed this church is believed to date from the late 700s. Certainly there was a church here long before the arrival of the Normans who subsequently built their own church on the spot. However that church collapsed suddenly in 1788 taking everyone in the town by surprise, except for the newly arrived engineer, Thomas Telford, who had predicted that its collapse was imminent. Once the rubble had been cleared away all that survived was the Lady Chapel which you can still see.

Believe it or not the inn was once linked to Old St Chad's by an arched passageway over what was then a much narrower street. The inn's name, Golden Cross, gives a clue as to its purpose. As an inn it would originally have housed visitors to the town who were here on church business. But it also served as the sacristy for the church where relics and vestments would have been kept.

Now continue along Princess Street until you reach the Square. Stop at the far side of the old Market Hall (beside *Jaeger's*) and look back at the building. The Market Hall has been recently restored and now serves as a coffee shop and cinema. It's unusual in that most market buildings used to hold markets only on the ground floor – this certainly happened here but the upper floor was also used for the town's woollen cloth market. It was the early trade in wool and woollen cloth that was to make Shrewsbury a wealthy town in medieval times. But, by the time this hall was built – the date on the coat of arms is 1596 – that trade had declined considerably in importance.

From here, look beyond the market hall to the left, at the statue of another of Shropshire's sons – Robert Clive. Clive was born in the village of Moreton Say in 1725 and, at the age of 17 or 18, went to India to serve as a clerk for the East India Company. He then joined the Company's army and was still aged only 32 when he won the Battle of Plassey in 1757, thereby ensuring that India became part of a future British Empire. Returning to England, Clive later served as MP for Shrewsbury and as Mayor.

Leave the Square by walking on along Market Street on the right; cross over Shoplatch at the bottom and bear left to walk around the town's modern market. On turning the corner you will see a large black and white building ahead, overlooking a car park – Rowley's House. This beautiful 16th century building currently houses Shrewsbury's museum and is well worth visiting with a fabulous collection, particularly, of Roman artefacts from nearby Wroxeter. But for the moment I want you to cross Barker Street on the left and walk up Claremont Hill, just to the right of the *Belstone Brasserie,* to New St Chad's Church at the top.

Built to replace Old St Chad's, this is a relatively modern church. It was completed in 1792 and its construction was influenced by the "new" technology of the Industrial Revolution with iron columns being used in parts of the building. Another thing that was revolutionary at the time was

the church's shape. The main body of the church is circular and this modern style did not go down at all well with Shrewsbury's population at the time.

From the church go and explore the churchyard and see if you can find a gravestone with the name "Ebenezer Scrooge" on it. It's a film prop left here after Charles Dickens's book, *The Christmas Carol,* was filmed in Shrewsbury in the 1980s.

Finally, cross the road and go and stand by the memorial to soldiers who fought in the Boer War. From here you can look out over the Quarry Park that leads down to the River Severn and see, on the far side, the buildings of the present-day Shrewsbury School. It's in the gardens here that, every August, the Shrewsbury Flower Show is held. With breaks only during the First and Second World Wars it is one of the oldest flower shows in the country, if not the world. Shrewsbury is often described as "the town of flowers" and this is a well-deserved description. As early as the 1690s the town's gardens were admired by Celia Fiennes, who travelled all over England at the time writing a journal as she went.

Anyone who loves Shrewsbury will tell you that this tour doesn't begin to do justice to the town. I hope, however, that (as with all the tours in this book) I've inspired you to explore the town more fully on your own. But, before you leave this spot, take time to go for a stroll in the gardens laid out below and seek out the memorial bust to Percy Thrower. In the minds of most people Percy Thrower is associated with BBC television gardening programmes and *Blue Peter*. But it was in Shrewsbury that he made his name becoming Park Superintendent here just after the Second World War and this garden is, perhaps, his best memorial.

Street names are often self-explanatory. It's pretty obvious what was once sold in Butcher Row, Fish Street, Milk Street and Horsefair – all names that survive in Shrewsbury today. Others that have now gone include Candle Lane and Swine Street. I'll leave it to you to guess what was sold in Grope Lane.

Wellington

The tour of Wellington starts from the churchyard beside the parish church of All Saints, to the north of the railway line.

Like so many other Shropshire towns, Wellington was already an established settlement in Anglo-Saxon times. The town is referred to in the Domesday Book of 1086 as *Walitone* and there are two possible explanations for this – either the settlement where Weola's people (or family) lived or else a settlement beside a *wea leah*, a religious grove with a yew tree.

When our pagan ancestors were converted to Christianity, the missionaries who converted them were extremely wise in their understanding of how hard it was for people to change the habits of generations overnight. Consequently, those missionaries very often built their new Christian churches on sites already associated in the minds of local people with religious practices. It's highly likely therefore, that, if the religious grove explanation of the town's name is the correct one, we are standing where that early grove would have been.

So this site may have been associated with religion for hundreds, even thousands, of years. Not that this is immediately apparent when you look at the church. It dates from 1790 replacing an earlier church that had been damaged during the Civil War in the 1600s – things obviously moved fast in Wellington in those days! By the time it was built, however, the Industrial Revolution had begun and new ways of using iron in buildings had been introduced so that George Steuart, the architect, used iron pillars in its construction – these are now hidden under plaster. Incidentally, in Steuart's other major church (New St Chad's in Shrewsbury), built at around the same time, he also used iron columns.

In recent years the town of Wellington has established an annual literary festival (it's held each October) and, following the walk, you will

Before leaving the churchyard take the time to look for the Corbett tomb that sits on the narrow stretch of grass between the church and the railway line. It's made or iron with some delightfully ornate decoration. Sadly, it's in dire need of restoration.

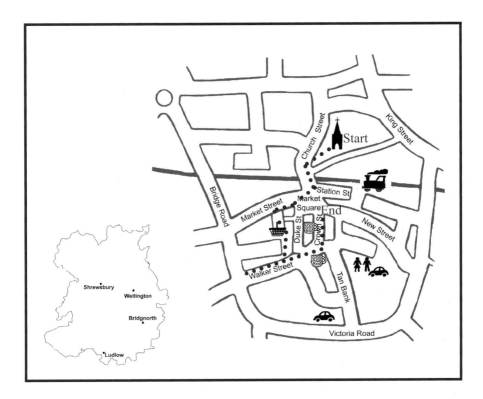

find that there are a number of great names in literature associated with the town. The first such name is that of Patrick Bronte, a young Irishman who served here as a curate from 1809. These days, of course, he is far better known as the father of the much more famous sisters Charlotte, Emily and Anne, but Patrick Bronte was the first of the family to publish work, in his case it was poetry.

Another curate at the church was Henry Gauntlett who lived here until 1814. His son, another Henry, was born in 1805 and grew up to become a leading organist and designer of organs. Henry Gauntlett wrote many hymns but today he is probably best known as the composer of the music for that favourite of Christmas carols, *Once in Royal David's City*.

Notice the sign over the entrance which reads "all the seats in this church are free and unappropriated for ever". This reminds us of the custom in the 18th and 19th century when families would buy the right to retain certain pews for their private use. Unless there were "free" pews, members of the congregation would otherwise have to stand where they could, even when there were pews vacant.

Leave the churchyard by walking through the lych gate, a memorial to the dead of the First and Second World Wars. In medieval times when someone died, the corpse wasn't coffined but was wrapped in a woollen shroud and carried to the church on a bier. The priest who conducted the funeral service then met the mourners at the entrance to the churchyard and conducted the funeral service, firstly at the gate and then by the graveside, not in the church at all as is the case today. The word *lych* comes from an Old English word meaning corpse. Incidentally, that shroud was an important source of income for the government which had passed a law insisting that all bodies be buried in woollen shrouds, wool being heavily taxed at the time. Wealthy people, wanting to show off their wealth, would be prepared to pay a fine for not using wool. At such times, with no coffin to hide the body, everyone attending the funeral would see that silk was being used instead.

Turning left you immediately cross over the railway line. Stop just beyond the bridge for a moment and look towards the station. The line,

which links Wellington with London and Shrewsbury, was built in 1849. Slicing through the town it cut the umbilical cord linking the church with the rest of Wellington so that now the northern side of the line is very much a quiet backwater compared with the trading town to the south. The railway went through more than just the town, it cut through the graveyard as well so that, in the course of building the line, many bodies were disinterred and moved. If you care to walk down on to the station platform you will notice a cross-shaped design within the ironwork. It's said locally that these are there to protect the station and the railway line from any ghosts disgruntled at the way in which their bodies were moved.

Cross over Station Road and look towards the Market Square. Today the open market area is much smaller than the original area used in 1244, when a charter to hold a regular market was conferred on the town. Try to imagine it as it then was with open land stretching to your left and ahead where now there are two rows of shops between Duke Street and Bell Street. There was also a large two-storey timber-framed market hall here with the town's Guildhall on the upper floor. Over time traders began to erect permanent stalls nearby and these evolved to become the rows of buildings that you see in front of you. It's a pattern that was repeated in many towns around the country.

We'll explore the streets ahead later on. For now I want you to go and stand beside the clock and look back towards the church. On your right there's a shop called Shoes in the Square with a blank plaque on the wall above. This was the birthplace in 1741 of William Withering, the son of an apothecary. Withering practised as a doctor (he was the highest earning doctor outside of London at the time) in Stafford and Birmingham and became a member of the Lunar Society, that great "think-tank" linking so many brilliant 18th century scientists and inventors. Tradition has it that Withering once met a wise woman in Shropshire who used foxgloves in her potions. All parts of the foxglove (*digitalis*) are highly poisonous but Withering discovered that it could be safely used in the treatment of heart conditions. He died in 1799 and is buried in Edgbaston in Birmingham.

Behind you, Thompson's Travel Agent is another link with Wellington's literary history. This was once the premises of Wellington's first bookshop, founded in the 1770s by Edward Houlston. In 1804 F Houlston & Son, as it was then known, began publishing books. The company was best known for the publication of sermons and religious tracts and, particularly, moralistic stories for children. They ceased trading in Wellington in the mid 1800s but the company continued in London until 1906.

From the clock, walk to your left along Market Street until you reach the entrance to Wellington Market. The 1244 charter was conferred on the local lords of the manor, the Forester family. In 1800 the Foresters dismantled and sold off the old market hall, leaving the local people with no covered area for their stalls so that, in 1856, a Market Company was formed, which purchased the ancient charter rights from the Forester family and, ten years later, built this market.

There is a market here every Tuesday, Thursday, Friday and Saturday so, if you are following this tour on one of those days do take the opportunity to walk through it and enjoy the atmosphere inside. With over 80 regular stalls it now extends as far as Walker Street. Wellington Market Company is one of Britain's largest such operators, running markets all over the country. It even has its share price quoted in the *Financial Times*. Stroll amongst the stalls until you emerge in Walker Street. (If the market is closed you will need to return to the Square, turn right into Duke Street and then right again into Walker Street.)

In medieval England the wool trade was all important. It was wool that made England wealthy and, to this day, the Chancellor of the Exchequer sits in the House of Lords on the *Woolsack*, a symbol of where England's wealth once came from. The name *Walker* is a reminder of this trade. When woollen cloth had been newly woven it was placed in large vats of liquid and then stamped on in order to matt the fibres together. The people who did this came to be known as walkers or fullers; hence Walker Street could once have been an area where this process was carried out.

Turn right when you leave the market and walk until you are opposite the library. Once the site of the town workhouse, there was later a brewery here and then, in 1902, the library was built. It was here in 1943 that Philip Larkin came to work. Born in 1922 Larkin had just graduated with first-class Honours from Oxford and his first job was as Librarian here in Wellington, a town with which he was not exactly enamoured at first and where he once complained that he spent most of his time "handing out tripey novels to morons". However, it was while he was here that he began working on

Ten Tree Croft
This little alleyway, leading off from Church Street just opposite All Saints, was originally known as Tentercroft. You have heard the phrase "to be on tenterhooks", meaning to be nervous or tense. It comes about because tenterhooks were once used to stretch woollen cloth that had just been woven and large areas of open ground known as "tentergrounds" were set aside for the practice.

his own novel, *A Girl in Winter* – it was published in 1947, by which time he had moved on to become Librarian at the University of Leicester. Larkin returned for a brief visit to the town in 1962 when he opened the extension to the library close to Larkin Way which, of course, was named for him.

From the library turn back towards the centre of town once more, keeping straight on into the pedestrian area when the road curves right. Go past Duke Street on the left and stop when you reach a pub called Rasputins. Once called the Raven, this is a lovely building with the prettiest of windows.

From Rasputins walk down Crown Street stopping beside another pub, the White Lion, Wellington's oldest pub. Across the street you will see the offices of the *Wellington News*. In 1642 King Charles I visited Wellington while raising his forces at the outbreak of the Civil War. He made a speech when he was here which came to be known as *The Wellington Declaration* in which he promised to uphold the laws of the country, the Protestant religion and the freedom of Parliament. It's not known exactly where he was when he made this speech (probably in either Orleton Park or Apley Castle). However, he is said to have stayed in the town in a building next to the Crown Inn in Crown Street – which would put him somewhere here.

Continue walking until you are once again in the Market Square; stop beside the old timber-framed building that now houses a sandwich bar. You are standing roughly on the spot where, in 1938, Sir Oswald Mosley once harangued a crowd of local people in an attempt to convert them to fascism – and caused a riot.

I would like to finish the tour by talking about another of Wellington's literary connections – Hesba Stretton, a writer whose name is virtually forgotten. Sarah Smith (to use her proper name) was born in 1832 in New Street, just to the right, in a house where her father ran the town's first post office. Stretton (she took the name from the town of Church Stretton whilst "Hesba" was invented from the initials of her brothers and sisters) started writing stories when she was still a child. Her first story was published in 1858 when her sister sent it off to Charles Dickens. Dickens liked it so much that he paid Stretton £5 and used it in a magazine he then edited. She was to become a regular contributor to the magazine.

Stretton's most famous book was *Jessica's First Prayer*, a somewhat mawkish, to modern tastes, story of a girl's discovery of the meaning of religion. The book was extremely popular at the time (it was published in 1867), being translated into many languages and selling at least two million copies. Hesba Stretton was particularly concerned with the plight of poor children in Victorian England so that today, although she's largely forgotten for her written work she should certainly be remembered and honoured for her role as a founder of the NSPCC.

Cecil and Malcolm Lawson

Cecil Lawson was born in Wellington in 1849. He was a painter of landscapes and flowers and already, by the age of 14, was earning a living through his art. Sadly, he was only just becoming famous when he died at the age of 32. His younger brother, Malcolm, was also born here. Malcolm grew up to achieve fame as a composer and arranger of traditional music, his most famous work being his arrangement of The Skye Boat Song.

Wem

The tour of Wem starts by the west door of St Peter's Church. Two thousand years ago this whole region would have been marshy with small hillocks, such as this one, dotted around the landscape. These would have been good places to settle. The surrounding marshland was perfect for hunting and fishing and also as a defence from any bands of marauders who may pass nearby. This also probably explains why the town is called Wem. In Anglo-Saxon times, by which time there was certainly a settlement of some sort here, it was named for the marshland that surrounded it. Wem simply meant a "stain" or "marsh".

Following his arrival in Shropshire soon after the Battle of Hastings, Roger de Montgomery gave lands, including this manor, to William Pantulf a man described by Montgomery's scribe as a "devout man, full of integrity". Mind you, Pantulf was later to be implicated in the murder of Montgomery's first wife but was vindicated after successfully undergoing a trial by fire, in other words walking on red-hot coals without harming himself!

Whatever the true story, it would have been on Pantulf's orders that the first castle was built. That castle was a wooden *motte and bailey* with the keep sitting on the motte or mound (peep over the wall into the garden next door and you can see all that remains of that mound).

Being a "devout man" it's quite possible that Pantulf was also responsible for the building of a church here to serve his castle garrison, if there wasn't one already on the site. No church is mentioned in the Domesday Book but it only listed those made of stone, not wooden ones.

On the church tower there's a carved, rather grim-faced figure – this is thought to be a later owner of the manor of Wem, Baron Ralph Greystock. The castle, the church and much of the town were destroyed in the 1400s during the Wars of the Roses after which Baron Greystock started a rebuilding programme. But he doesn't seem to have done much work on the castle because it was described soon afterwards as being in a ruinous state.

Bloody Judge Jeffreys

One famous person associated with Wem was "Bloody" Judge Jeffreys who owned nearby Lowe Hill Farm. Jeffreys, who was born in Wrexham and educated at Shrewsbury School, bought the Barony of Wem. I'm not sure that his is an association to be proud of – he became known as the Hanging Judge *when he presided over court cases in the south-west of England following the Monmouth Rebellion in 1685; those rebels not hung usually ended up as slaves on plantations in the West Indies.*

From the churchyard walk south, down some steps and into Mill Street. Turn right when you reach Barnard Street and then almost immediately turn right into Castle Court behind the terrace houses. Walk through the gate at the end of the street and stop just beyond.

Standing here it is much easier to recognise Wem's castle because you can now clearly see the former moat, where the vegetable gardens are. The northern line of the moat is obscured by buildings but the curve of the road beyond (today's High Street) defines where the boundary of the castle once was.

Walk on to the High Street, cross the road beyond and stop so that you can look back the way you have come. The first thing to catch your eye will probably be the timber framed house on the corner with its brick façade. This is typical of many town houses all over England where fake facades were added as occupants wanted to aggrandise their properties. In this instance, however, the distinction between the two is clear to see.

Continue walking westwards. Today this is still part of High Street. Once, though, it was known as Old Cripple Street – possibly because it was along here that beggars making for the Poor House (at this end of the town) would have made their way.

Look out as you go for the fire station on the right and, when you reach it, look through the glass doors. Displayed on the wall is an enormous iron hook – hooks like this were used to pull down the thatched roofs or entire walls of houses in order to try and prevent the spread of fire. This fire hook was used in the Great Fire of Wem in 1677 but, sadly, that fire was too fierce and it didn't really save the town at all.

Once past the fire station turn right into Noble Street. Perhaps it is so-called because we are now standing at the edge of the medieval town and people coming to market would have had to pay a *noble* (around 33p) to trade here. Originally this street was known as Back Street which explains its purpose much better, as it marked the original outer limit of the town.

Having turned into Noble Street stop opposite Adams School. The school was founded in 1650 by Sir Thomas Adams, son of a landowner and tanner, who once lived on this site. Adams left Wem to study at Cambridge and from there he went to London where he became a successful and wealthy member of the Draper's Guild of London, also becoming Lord

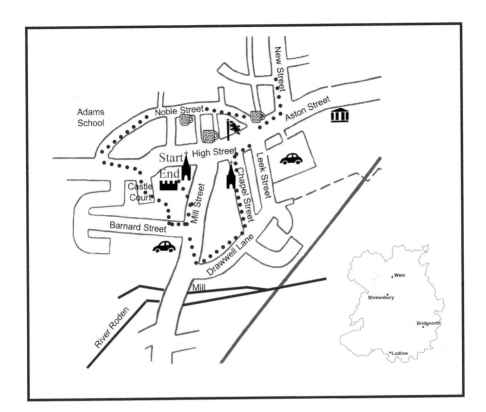

Mayor of London in 1646. He was a staunch Royalist and was imprisoned by Parliamentarians in the Tower of London for a time. However, with the return of Charles II to the throne his fortunes revived and he became a Baronet. This school wasn't his only educational establishment – he also founded a Chair of Arabic at Cambridge.

Adams's death in 1668 was mentioned by Samuel Pepys in his diary – Pepys described how a gallstone weighing 25 ounces was removed from Adams's body; it's now preserved in a laboratory in Cambridge.

As you walk along Noble Street look out for the three storey building on the right with the strange looking shuttering. A little beyond it is Tannery Court and this gives a clue to what went on here. As a largely rural county,

Shropshire has dozens of reminders that the tanning of leather was a major local industry and this building was used for drying skins. That slatted wall is now nailed tight but once the slats would have been loose and could have been moved up or down in order to control the flow of air through the building.

Noble Street contains a fine mixture of styles and periods of houses, most of them dating from after the 1677 fire. However, there are two cottages here, on the left near the Dickin Arms, that survived – this was as far as the fire came.

Further along Noble Street there's an open car park on the right, behind the White Horse pub. Notice the odd brick building with the little church-like window to the side - it was once a Unitarian chapel, built in 1716. It was here that the Revd William Hazlitt served as a minister. He lived in the white house next door and his son, another William Hazlitt, was educated at Adams School, growing up to become a famous essayist and writer. Hazlitt's best known work is probably his *Characters of Shakespeare's plays* published in 1817, which has been a useful crib for students of Shakespeare ever since.

Another famous Wemian was John Astley who was born in 1727 and lived in the timber house at No 4. Astley was an artist who gained an excellent reputation as a portrait painter. At one point in his life he earned £3,000 over a period of just three years – a phenomenal sum for the times.

Returning to the High Street, turn left and then left again into New Street. New Street was new in the 1500s, when the medieval town was expanding beyond its original boundaries. But the town retracted somewhat during the Civil War when the buildings here were pulled down as a defensive measure.

Once the street would have been dominated by New Hall on the other side of the road, now almost lost behind the garage. Built in the late 1700s New Hall later became the home of Sir John Bickerton Williams who was the first man to be knighted by Queen Victoria.

Retrace your steps and return to the High Street. The small group of shops on your right are known as the Maypole, getting their name from Aston Street, previously known as Maypole End, because there was once a maypole nearby.

Just before you reach the Castle pub on the High Street, walk down the little lane beside it and look into the yard behind. At the far end you will see a brick arch with the word "Smithfield" carved on it. This was once an entrance to the livestock market beyond. Cattle and pigs were sold here. In fact it was once well known that "Shropshire hogs are the best in England".

Back on the main street, cross the road at the pedestrian crossing and continue until you are standing opposite a sweet shop called the *Wem Treacle Mine*. Its name comes from an old tradition that there were once treacle mines in Wem. Of course, there are no such things but Wem with its brewing industry (Wem ales were famous throughout the Midlands) and its tanneries, produced prodigious amounts of waste that is sticky and gooey – treacly, in fact.

One story has it that long, long ago someone in the town collected this *treacle* in some barrels which he stored in his cellar. Years later he rediscovered the barrels, opened one, tasted the mixture inside and rather liked it. And so he sold it as a cure-all medicine. It was extremely popular. Whether or not it cured people's ills is debatable but for those who didn't recover, there's another saying in Wem that they "went down the treacle mines" and never returned!

Next door is the Town Hall. The building you are looking at is a Victorian façade on the front of a modern building rebuilt following a fire in 1995. Today the Town Hall is the focus for Wem's weekly market. The first charter for a market here was obtained from King John. In those days the market was held on a Sunday but some years later Sunday markets were banned by the Pope and so, in 1351, market day was changed to Thursday.

The Great Fire of 1677 was disastrous for trade in the town and it was over 50 years before Wem recovered. The Town Hall is said to be haunted by the ghost of Jane Churm, the 14 year-old who started it. Jane had gone into the attic of a cottage nearby carrying her lit candle, the flame caught the thatch and almost the entire town burnt as a result. Just inside the entrance to the Town Hall is a plaque commemorating that earlier fire.

Now turn to your left and walk down Chapel Street. The site where the fire started is thought to be occupied by No 5, on the left; later there was a Primitive Methodist Chapel here. Further down the street there's a Baptist chapel. These two chapels explain the street's name. It's a little confusing since, in the old books, the fire is described as starting in Leek Street. Today Leek Street is the next street along, (you crossed over it as you walked down the High Street). In Jane's time it was known as Dark Lane and marked the eastern boundary of the town.

Chapel Street is another attractive street with a variety of building styles. There's the former British School on the left - you can see the name carved in the arch above the alleyway. It would have cost one penny a day to send your child here to learn to read; reading and writing cost tuppence and three pence a day would have paid for your child to learn "other accomplishments" as well.

Further along is the old Victorian police station. That large station was manned by one sergeant and one constable and survived as a police station until the 1960s.

Then there's the delightfully named Tally Ho Cottage. It's not so much the architecture that is of interest (note the iron-framed windows) but someone who lived here. The house was occupied in the 1800s by William Henry Betty. He was a child actor who, in 1804, aged twelve, could command £100 for a single performance. A detachment of guards had to be posted outside the theatre to preserve order amongst his fans – it all sounds so familiar! He retired at the age of 16 with a handsome fortune, became bored with retirement and returned to the stage only to flop totally. He then retired once again and lived here in Wem.

At the end of Chapel Street turn right into Drawwell Lane. You are now walking beside the line of the southern walls of the town although any evidence of those walls is lost under later houses and gardens.

The women of Wem and a few musketeers
Beat off Lord Capel and all his Cavaliers.

The Civil War of the 1600s affected all parts of the country and Wem was no exception. By and large, Shropshire supported the Royalist cause. Wem, however, supported Parliament. In 1643 a garrison was formed to defend the town from attack – it was at this time that houses beyond the town walls were destroyed. But when the attack came not only were the defences incomplete but the town's garrison of only 40 men were no match to the besieging force of (it's said) 5,000. These few soldiers and an undisciplined rabble of men and women defended the town – they put on red capes and marched up and down the ramparts to give the impression that there were more soldiers than in fact there were. In the end the attacking force gave up.

The following year it seemed there would be a second attack but this time Prince Rupert decided Wem wasn't worth it, saying "It's a crow's nest that would not afford each of my men a piece of bread".

At the end of Drawwell Lane just over the bridge on the left is the mill. Newly converted into apartments, the core of the old mill survives. We know there has been a mill on this site since Norman times because one early document relates how land at Sleap was given to one of William Pantulf's knights on condition he helped to build the castle at Wem and brought his corn to this mill.

Notice the tall chimney. It was built in the 1820s when a steam engine was installed so that the mill could run even when there was no water in the river. The local people complained bitterly at this. It wasn't that they feared it would take work from them; in fact their complaint was the very modern one that they were worried about the pollution it would cause!

Walk up Mill Street to return to the church. Stop just as you enter the churchyard. The only part of the early church to survive the Great Fire was the tower. The church was rebuilt within a year using money raised from donations sent from all over the country. Unfortunately it appears to have been rather shoddy workmanship so that by the 1800s it was in very poor condition and described as being "the ugliest and worst ventilated building in the Diocese".

Incidentally, when he heard of the Great Fire, a former vicar of Wem living in London wrote to the local people deploring the fire but also said that such events were a judgement on people for their wickedness. The same thing happened when Bridgnorth had its fire – those 17th century churchmen could be an unforgiving lot!

To finish the tour walk to the other side of the church so that you overlook the busy road junction. That first Norman castle was sited here to control the junction and it's been a bottleneck ever since. Try to imagine it, however, with an additional row of houses between the church and the main road because that is what was here until 1941 when the Union Buildings, as they were known, were demolished – their cellars are still under the road.

The Mythstories Museum is the world's first museum of myths and legends. Shropshire, with its plethora of such stories, is the perfect place to find such a museum.

Whitchurch

The tour of Whitchurch begins in the car park beside Newtown (the name of the road next to the car park). Whitchurch is the oldest town in Shropshire, dating from Roman times. The only other Roman town in the county worthy of the name was Wroxeter, but it was abandoned sometime in the 6th century. Whitchurch, however, has been continuously occupied.

Believe it or not, here in the car park you are standing within the Roman town of *Mediolanum*, a staging point between *Viroconium* (Wroxeter) and *Deva* (Chester). Nothing remains of that ancient settlement; however, burial urns have been found on either side of the road coming into the town from the south where the present day Sedgeford (Road) roughly follows the line of the Roman road.

The first Romans established a fort here around the end of the first century AD and it covered the area between here, Pepper Street to the south, a line behind the houses on the western side of the High Street and Yardington to the north. Then, as the Romans took control over all of Britannia, their armies moved northwards and, as at Wroxeter, this fort developed into a town.

Now walk from the car park, turning left in Newtown and then right when you reach Yardington. Stop when you reach the junction with Bargates.

Sir John Talbot

There's a plaque beside the door of St Alkmund's Church that recalls Sir John Talbot. Described by William Shakespeare in his play, *Henry VI, Part 1*, as "the scourge of France", Sir John gained a reputation fighting with Henry V at battles such as Agincourt.

At one time Sir John held the town of Neufchatel-en-Bray, a link that survives to this day as that town is now twinned with Whitchurch. Holding Rouen when it was captured by the French, Sir John became their prisoner. He was released on condition that he went on a pilgrimage to Rome and never again wore armour if fighting the French. This was to be his undoing because, fighting once more against the French but not wearing armour, he was easily killed.

In his will Sir John Talbot asked to be buried here and his heart was embalmed and brought back to Whitchurch and buried in a silver casket.

Someone else who was, very briefly, buried here was Harry Hotspur. Hotspur was killed at the Battle of Shrewsbury in 1403 fighting against Henry IV. He was buried here by his cousin, Lord Furnival, but the king then demanded that his body should be disinterred and brought to Shrewsbury where it could be displayed before being hung, drawn and quartered.

On the right there's a garden area with a long, low wall beside it. The wall follows the line, discovered in excavations in 1976, of the northern limit of the Roman town. Officially, the Romans abandoned Britannia in AD 410 when Rome itself was threatened by invaders. For a time the people here would have continued to live much as normal but, one by one, many of the old towns were abandoned. Somehow Mediolanum survived so that over 600 years later, when England was once again invaded, this time by the Normans, there was still a settlement here.

Like the Romans before, the Normans wanted to control their newly conquered territories. In order to do this, they built castles and that was exactly what they did when they came to *Westune*, as the Saxons by then called this settlement.

The Normans built their castle on the highest part of the hill, somewhere here. Apart from the name Castle Hill at the bottom of Newtown, hardly a trace of the Norman castle remains today. Incidentally, the name Newtown came about some centuries later when, the castle having been abandoned, the site was used for the further development of the town.

Cross the road beside the Greyhound pub and walk a short way down Bargates, stopping opposite the almshouse dedicated to Samuel Higginson.

It seems strange at first that the present town has shifted from the original Roman site. However, once the Normans had built their castle there was no way they would allow ordinary people to follow the route of the old road right through it. And so the medieval town grew up alongside the castle. Here you are close to the site of one of the medieval town gates, known still as Bargates.

Samuel Higginson founded the almshouses across the road in the late 1600s to house six "decayed housekeepers". Next door is another, smaller building with a plaque that recalls Samuel's wife, Jane, who left money in her will for the endowment of a schoolhouse for the teaching of poor children. Apparently the endowment also ensured that the schoolmaster here

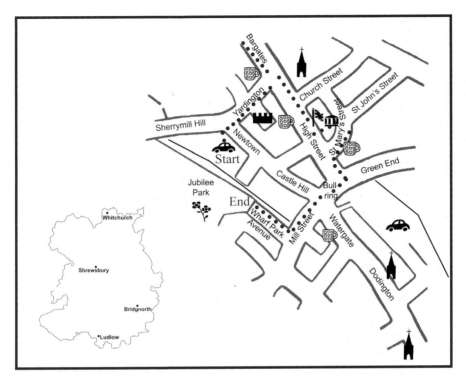

could be given an annual salary of £10 "to him and his successors for ever". This charming Queen Anne style house is now privately owned.

Further down the hill, just beyond Jane's schoolhouse, is another former school. Although very much in the Tudor style the building dates from 1848. Now converted into flats it was once the old Free Grammar School, founded originally in the 1500s. "Free" in this context meant that it was free from interference by the church. The school closed in 1938.

Retrace your steps and cross the road to reach the entrance to St Alkmund's Church.

The church sits outside the boundaries of the original Roman settlement which would seem to indicate that already, in Saxon times, when the first church was built here, Westune had stretched beyond the Roman boundaries. Alkmund was a Christian prince murdered around the year 800 by the man who had usurped his father's throne. The Saxon church dedicated to him was replaced in around 1085, soon after the Norman Conquest. That 11th century church was built of Grinshill stone which, when newly cut from the quarry, looks very white and this may be how the town came to be known as "White-church".

The Norman church was replaced around 1350. It then collapsed in 1711. So that the one you see today is the fourth church here. Take time if you can to go inside. Consecrated in 1713, it cost £4,000 to build and your first impression as you enter the church is surprise at its spaciousness – it is one of the largest in Shropshire. Then, as you leave St Alkmund's, take time to look at the rather fine collection of iron tombstones next to the pathway.

Cross over Church Street and walk into High Street. The High Street follows the line of the medieval road from Shrewsbury to Chester. The road is much narrower now than it was then as this would have been an area for markets with space required for both livestock and stalls. In fact, the frontages of many of the houses, particularly those on the right, originally stood further back but have encroached onto the road over the years.

This does mean, sadly, that the most interesting features of many of the houses that you pass are often hidden within the structure. Furthermore, like so many other towns in Shropshire, Whitchurch suffered regular attacks from the Welsh. One of these, in 1404, resulted in a severe fire damaging much of the town. Consequently the oldest buildings tend to date from the period of rebuilding after that fire.

Walk down the street and pause when you are opposite the Red Lyon pub. Briefly renamed the Victorian during the 1800s, the Red Lyon used to be famous for the cockfights that were held behind the building. I particularly like the story about a Whitchurch schoolmaster who was dismissed when it was discovered that he was allowing his schoolboys to bet on the outcome of cockfights.

Continue along the street until you reach the Town Hall which sits back from the road, on your left. Look across the road at the building with the unusual iron decoration around its first floor windows. There was once another inn on this site, namely the Crown, that was subsequently used for JB Joyce's clock factory.

JB Joyce is the most famous company in Whitchurch. It was founded in 1690 in Ellesmere by James Joyce and moved to Whitchurch a hundred years later. In 1830 (by which time the company was known as JB Joyce after John Barnett Joyce) they began producing tower clocks and then employed between 15 and 20 engineers. Today the factory occupies premises in Station Road, moving there in 1904. JB Joyce clocks can be found all over the world. Next time you check the time at a railway station anywhere in the UK, see if the clock was made by them – chances are that it was.

Further down the street, this time on the left hand side, is Walkers Bakery. Parts of this delightful building date from the mid 1400s, although it was much altered in the 1600s. It was yet another pub – the Swan. Notice the lovely stained glass decoration over the shop windows.

Take care as you pass Walkers that you don't miss the little alleyway beyond, where you turn left into Bluegates. The name is a puzzle because this was never a main gateway but just a little lane linking the High Street with the alleyways that served the buildings from the back. Perhaps the gates at the entrance were once painted blue.

Bluegates leads to a craft centre and the Whitchurch Heritage Centre. The building was originally a Wesleyan Methodist Chapel, later an auctioneer's office and then it became the town's post office. There are fascinating exhibits linked to JB Joyce within.

From the Heritage Centre walk down the hill along St Mary's Street to return to the High Street, stopping when you reach the Old Town Hall Vaults pub. This was where the composer, Sir Edward German, was born in 1862. His grandfather was a brewer and his father ran this pub. Famous for his light operas, his best known works are *Tom Jones* and *Merrie England*, the latter being written for the Savoy Theatre in 1902. Sir Edward was knighted in 1928 and died in 1936. He is buried here in Whitchurch.

Stop once more when you reach High Street. There's a branch of the National Westminster Bank just across the road. In the 1500s there was yet another pub, the Angel, on this site. Notice the heavy front doors on the bank – they are thought to have come from the old St Alkmund's after it fell down.

Cross the road and walk to the bottom of the High Street to stand beside the clock. It will be no surprise to learn that this was made by JB Joyce. The four sides display the different names of the town through its history – Mediolanum, Westune, Album Monasterium ("the white church" in Latin, a name used in medieval documents) and, of course, Whitchurch.

The clock stands in the Bull Ring, so-called because this was where bull fights took place, the last one being staged in 1802. Bull rings always needed to be large open areas where lots of people could congregate, sites that invariably were also used as markets and this one is no exception. John Leland, writing in around

1540 mentioned that "the tounne of Whitchurch hath a veri good market", a comment that Daniel Defoe, visiting in the late 1600s, was to endorse.

Whitchurch was granted a charter to hold a market by Richard I at the end of the 12th century. Then in 1362 a further charter was given, granting a licence to hold a fair for three days every year "on the eve, the feast and the morrow of St Simon and St Jude" – in other words on 27, 28 and 29 October. This whole area would have been used for the market with stalls extending along the High Street as well. In 1638 the town's first Market House was built – described as a place where "poore people may sit in the dry and sell butter, cheese and other commodity".

From here walk to the far end of the Bull Ring and stop so that you can see along Watergate, which lies straight ahead. This is another name that reminds us where the town's medieval boundaries once were. The pedestrian area between the clock and this spot links Castle Hill and the High Street and presumably dates from medieval times when, from here, people would take one of two routes, either to the castle or through the town.

The fire that was caused by the Welsh attack in 1404 would seem not to have reached this part of town since the Old Eagles pub (on the right in Watergate) is thought to be the oldest building in the town, parts of it dating from 1400.

From the Bull Ring walk ahead into Mill Street. Whitchurch once had four mills serving the town, one of which, the Town Mill, was situated here. That fire in 1404 may have missed the Old Eagles but it destroyed this mill. Welsh raids were a constant problem for Shropshire in the 1300s and 1400s, only coming to an end with the accession to the throne of the Tudor (Welsh) king, Henry VII in 1485. Quite often various towns would make individual truces with the Welsh and apparently this had happened with a number of towns in northern Shropshire in the early 1400s; Whitchurch, didn't join the truce on that occasion and so Whitchurch was burnt.

Walk along Mill Street and turn right into Wharf Park Avenue; stop when you reach the entrance to Jubilee Park. This is where our tour of Whitchurch ends.

This part of Whitchurch hasn't always been so peaceful. The main route of the Ellesmere Canal went past Whitchurch about a mile to the north west and so a branch line was added reaching Sherrymans Bridge (now known as Sherrymill Hill) at the other end of the park in 1808. Subsequently this area was developed with a wharf and warehouses. Goods brought into the town included coal, lime and iron and from here boots and shoes and cheese were sent out. Coal coming from Ruabon was used to produce gas and a gas works was built on the site of the car park (on the hill to the right) where the tour began. The gas works was demolished in the 1970s.

In the meantime a field adjacent to the canal was bought by public subscription to celebrate Queen Victoria's Golden Jubilee in 1887. At first it was little more than an open area for the public to use but with the closing of the canal it was developed into the parkland you see today. In recent years a section of the branch line linking with the Ellesmere Canal (or Shropshire Union Canal as it is now known) has been restored and it's hoped that perhaps before too long the canal will be restored all the way into Whitchurch.

Positioned within the wall of houses in Mill Street is this curious feature with the initials "W" and "D" on it. It marks the boundary between the parishes of Whitchurch and Dodington.

Dorothy Nicolle will tell you that she has the perfect job - she lives in Shropshire where she is a professional (Blue Badge) tourist guide for the Heart of England region. This means she can constantly share her love of exploring Britain and its history with visitors and local people alike.

She regularly leads tours throughout the area (both coach tours and walking tours), although she tends to concentrate her guiding in Shropshire and the immediate surrounding counties.

Dorothy also lectures on a variety of subjects, mainly to do with history. She is particularly interested in the hidden history of subjects we otherwise take for granted - pub signs or nursery rhymes, the English language or even Christmas.

For further information about her tours and lectures please visit her website at www.nicolle.me.uk

Books by Dorothy Nicolle

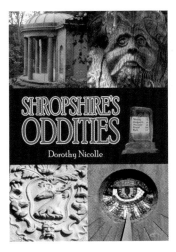

Shropshire's oddities is a selection of unusual things to be found around the county. Discovering each new oddity is like winning a prize in a quirky type of treasure hunt and, before long you will find yourself seeing Shropshie with fresh eyes.
Price £12.99

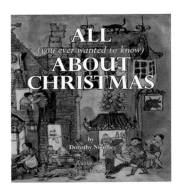

All (you ever wanted to know) about Christmas explores the myths and traditions that surround the festive season. It answers all the questions you ever asked about Christmas and many that you never even thought of. This book explains it all.
Price £5.99

To order a copy of one of the above books please send your cheque or postal order, made out to 'Dorothy Nicolle' to:
Dorothy Nicolle, 32 Chapel Street, Wem, Shropshire SY4 5ER.
Postage is included in the price of each book to addresses within the UK.

Children's books by Dorothy Nicolle

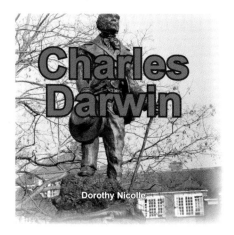

When he was a youngster Darwin struggled at school and no-one ever expected he would become one of the finest scientists of his age. *Charles Darwin* is an inspiring book for young people and is aimed at children of 6 or 7.
Price £5.99

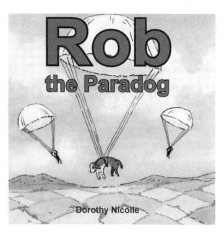

The true story of Rob, an ordinary farm dog who served in the army during the Second World War and won the Dickin Medal (the animals' VC) for his courage. *Rob the Paradog* is an easy-reader book for children aged 6 or 7.
Price £5.99

Blue Hills Press

To order a copy of one of the above books please send your cheque or postal order, made out to 'Dorothy Nicolle' to:
Dorothy Nicolle, 32 Chapel Street, Wem, Shropshire SY4 5ER.
Postage is included in the price of each book to addresses within the UK.